FROM
freezer
to TABLE

FROM freezer to TABLE

75+ SIMPLE, WHOLE FOODS RECIPES
for Gathering, Cooking, and Sharing

POLLY CONNER
& RACHEL TIEMEYER

RODALE

RODALE
wellness

Live happy. Be healthy. Get inspired.

Sign up today to get exclusive access to our authors, exclusive bonuses,
and the most authoritative, useful, and cutting-edge information on health,
wellness, fitness, and living your life to the fullest.

Visit us online at RodaleWellness.com
Join us at RodaleWellness.com/Join

Rodale books may be purchased for business or promotional use or for special sales. For information, please e-mail
rodalebooks@rodale.com.

Printed in China
Rodale Inc. makes every effort to use acid-free ♾, recycled paper ♲.

Food photographs by Mitch Mandel/Rodale Images
Food styling by Lisa Homa
Prop styling by Stephanie Hanes

Lifestyle photographs by Scott Patrick Myers Photography

Clock icon: Voodoo Dot/Shutterstock; carrot and dish icons: Line Icons by freebird/Shutterstock;
child icon by musmellow/Shutterstock

Book design by Rae Ann Spitzenberger

Library of Congress Cataloging-in-Publication Data is on file with the publisher.

ISBN 978-1-62336-894-4   paperback

Distributed to the trade by Macmillan

2 4 6 8 10 9 7 5 3 1

We inspire health, healing, happiness, and love in the world.
Starting with you.

To our husbands and families: *You're our biggest cheerleaders and the most honest recipe testers we'll ever find. We love you. So much.*

· · · · · · · · · · · · · · · · ·

To our dear friends: *You keep us upright.
We are grateful for you in our lives.*

· · · · · · · · · · · · · · · · ·

To our Thriving Home readers: *What a faithful tribe you are.
You got us to this point, and you keep us going.*

CONTENTS

Polly

Rachel

Introduction

RACHEL'S STORY

It was 2007 and I was floundering. I had just had my first baby, a sweet little boy, and I'd made the decision to stay home full-time with him. So our one-income budget was tight. My time was tight. And to be honest, my post-pregnancy jeans were tight. It seemed like the only thing that had room to grow was my cooking repertoire. I just could not get dinner figured out.

Before kids, I had this lovely vision of providing healthy, homemade meals at the dinner table each evening as my husband walked through the door. As you can probably guess, that never happened. Not even close. I couldn't wrap my mind around how I was supposed to cook with a fussy baby in tow. Plus, how could we possibly afford fresh, whole foods on our now shrunken, one-income grocery budget? And where was I supposed to find recipes that my family would actually like, much less ones that were also easy and nutritious? So, most nights, I would throw my hands up, open the freezer, and pull out a processed frozen pizza or boxed lasagna. We weren't eating well, and I didn't have a clue what to do about it.

That is, until my friend Darcie invited me to join her Freezer Club in the spring of that same year. I remember our first meeting well: At a cluster of tables at our favorite coffee shop with printouts of recipes in hand, some of my girlfriends and I excitedly hashed out our first monthly menu of freezer meals (ones that can be easily frozen for later use). We were ready to conquer the great dinner hour divide!

At our second meeting, about a month later, we all swapped the frozen meals we had worked so hard making for each other the previous month on our own time. I came home that night, filled my freezer with 12 ready-to-go, homemade dinners, and was hooked! This new concept of freezer cooking with friends was a huge breakthrough for our family.

POLLY'S STORY

A few years down the road, I would find myself facing a similar dinnertime struggle as Rachel did before she started her freezer club. As my husband spent many evenings in night classes, I quickly learned that juggling tired kids alone didn't allow much time for cooking and put a damper on this extrovert's social life.

After dabbling in freezer cooking on my own, a big turning point came when I participated in a Freezer Cooking Party. For the first time I had a freezer full of easy-to-prepare and wholesome meals for the nights when I didn't have the time or energy to cook. It was ah-maz-ing! That one-time event was the motivation I needed to fully embrace the benefits of this lifestyle. I began to double and freeze meals regularly and even rallied friends to have more Freezer Cooking Parties.

Then, this past year, my friends and I finally began our own ongoing Freezer Club. With these changes, we now eat out less, I have lowered our grocery bill, and I have also benefited from the much-needed time with friends. Similar to Rachel, I have lost weight as my diet has changed, and I've grown to love cooking from scratch using whole food ingredients. Freezer cooking is now a foundational way I feed my family.

OUR NEW LIFESTYLE

For both of us, freezer cooking was no passing fad or newfangled diet. Rather, it became a lifestyle that continues to be a time-saver, money-saver, waistline-saver, and sanity-saver during some intensely busy years. One of the most surprising benefits we've found along the way was the formation of lasting friendships with the people we partnered to cook with. Having a reason to regularly gather together with our girlfriends ended up being a source of refreshment and companionship that was much needed in those "little years" of staying home with our young children. Who knew stocking our freezers could be so much fun and foster deep friendships at the same time?

Our blog, Thriving Home, which we began together in 2012, aims to equip readers to create flourishing homes. When we began sharing freezer cooking tips and recipes there years ago, they quickly rose to the top as our most popular posts. As Thriving Home became a go-to site for healthy freezer cooking, readers began requesting that we write a freezer meal cookbook. It was at this point that we decided to create this ultimate resource to help anyone—no matter their age or stage—experience the breakthrough at home that we did.

Our genuine hope is that *From Freezer to Table* will result in a positive lifestyle shift for you, too, and that you become inspired and equipped to make freezer cooking a way of life. Whether you form your own Freezer Club, throw Freezer Cooking Parties, or just learn to do freezer cooking on your own, we believe the concepts and recipes in our book will help you enjoy healthy, delicious, stress-free meals around the table with those you love most.

OUR RECIPES

We get it. You're hesitant about freezer cooking, right? Maybe you've had a bad experience with it in the past, or have a notion that freezer meals are bland, mushy, and beige, or that this book is only full of casseroles (not that there's anything wrong with a good casserole!). Well, we're here to shatter all those preconceived ideas.

We know that freezer meals can taste just as good as a fresh meal when prepared correctly. And we know that they can be full of vibrant color and complex flavors, too. Honestly, *From Freezer to Table* was written as much for ourselves as for you. That means every recipe in here is one that we are proud of and make again and again in our own homes. In fact, we worked hard to make sure all of our recipes met these four goals:

▶ **Delicious:** We aren't here to waste anyone's time. If a recipe wasn't one that our own families and our recipe testing team didn't enjoy, it simply didn't make the cut. Like you, if we're going to spend time cooking, we want some yummy food on the table! So deliciousness was our first and most important goal.

▶ **Whole Foods:** What makes our recipes stand out from freezer meals you might find elsewhere is that they are primarily made with whole food ingredients. Each one reflects our commitment to the "whole foods philosophy," where cooking at home, carefully selecting all-natural ingredients, and eating a variety of vegetables and fruits, whole grains,

healthy fats, and local or organic meats are the foundation of a healthy diet.

▶ **Freezer-Friendly:** Although every recipe in here was created and tested as a (delicious) fresh meal, it also had to pass the (delicious) freezer-friendly test. That means it must freeze, thaw, and prepare safely and well, with no major textural or taste changes along the way. To make it easy for you, we've included simple freezer meal instructions at the bottom of every recipe.

▶ **Easy to Prepare:** If you're reading this book, we know you have a packed schedule. As much as you may love cooking (or not), your time is precious. So we've intentionally chosen recipes that are simple enough for anyone to make. We tried to find the shortest path to the best result in every single one.

Throughout the book, we also included icons to guide you to recipes that meet your specific needs and lifestyles:

🕐 *30 Minutes or Less:* Just because you're cooking in bulk and stocking the freezer doesn't mean it needs to be a big production. These recipes can be done from start to finish in under 30 minutes, so you can spend more time with the people you love most in your life.

👤 *Kid Favorite:* Got a picky eater on your hands? Want a meal that you know kids will gobble up with no complaints? We've got your back. We've gone through and identified the recipes that have proven to be no-fail meals for children.

Sneaky Nutrition: Because we know the struggle of getting the recommended amount of fruits and vegetables on our plates every day, we have found all sorts of ways to include extra nutrition in our recipes. The good news is that our sneaky methods don't affect the taste or texture. Shhh—don't tell your kids!

Gluten-Free: Gluten-free doesn't have to mean taste-free. We've flagged many great options that will not only make your gluten-free eater happy but are sure to satisfy everyone else at the dinner table as well.

Grab and Go: When the pace of life is fast, eating healthy is often the first thing kicked to the curb. By keeping a stash of grab-and-go meals in the freezer, you can avoid the drive-thru and have healthy options to grab while running out the door.

Take to Others: One of the best parts of freezer cooking is that you can always have a meal on hand for a friend or neighbor in need. From breakfast favorites and the best comforting casseroles to gluten-free meals, you'll find many of our top picks for the meals we regularly give to others.

HOW TO USE THIS BOOK

This may be the most versatile cookbook you own, and here's why. Whether you want to make a healthy, family-friendly dinner for tonight *or* make a few freezer meals on your own this weekend for future breakfasts, lunches, or dinners, this book is for you. Whether you want to try freezer cooking with friends at a Freezer Cooking Party *or* form an ongoing Freezer Club, this book is for you. We're going to provide you with the motivation and tools to cook simple, tasty, whole foods meals anytime *and* help you implement the freezer cooking lifestyle in whatever way works best for you.

So read on and take our hands as we walk you through the basics of freezer cooking on your own or with friends. Take a deep breath, because you'll be enjoying healthy, homemade meals from freezer to table regularly!

HOW MUCH DO YOU KNOW ABOUT FREEZER COOKING?

Remember those quizzes you took in teen magazines long ago to learn something *crucial* about yourself? You know, like "What's your prom dress style?" or "What kind of flirt are you?" Surprise! We have a pop quiz for you, too. Hopefully this one's a little more useful but still fun!

Before we help you kick-start your new lifestyle, let's take note of where you currently are on the freezer cooking spectrum, shall we? Answer the questions below to find out how much you actually know about freezer cooking.

1. **Most frozen food can remain safely frozen for:**
   a. 3 months
   b. 12 months
   c. Like, forever!
   d. Ladies, I have no clue. That's why I bought this book.

2. **Which of the following food items do not freeze safely? (Circle all that apply.)**
   a. Eggs in shell
   b. Tomatoes
   c. Canned food (still in cans)
   d. Mayonnaise

3. **Freezing homemade meals destroys:**
   a. All bacteria and parasites that might be in the food (gross, right?)
   b. Nutrients in the food
   c. Everything I like about good food
   d. None of the above

4. **According to food safety experts, what temperature should your freezer register at all times to keep food safe?**
   a. 32°F
   b. 15°F
   c. 0°F
   d. Any of the above will freeze food safely.

5. **True or False? It is safe to freeze meat or poultry directly in its original store packaging.**

6. In 15 seconds, can you name three safe methods for thawing frozen food? (Put your phone down—no cheating!) Ready, go!

_____

_____

_____

_____

_____

7. True or False? Once a food has been frozen and thawed, you cannot freeze it again.

8. The coldest spot in the freezer is:

   a. Right next to the vent where the cold air comes out. Duh.

   b. Since cold air sinks, it's the bottom shelf of any freezer. Duh.

   c. The ice box. It's filled with ice. Duh.

   d. The rear center. It's the most insulated point. Duh.

9. Which of these is an advantage of hosting a Freezer Cooking Party or being in a Freezer Club?

   a. You'll save money. Woo-hoo!

   b. You get to hang out with friends while accomplishing a task. Cheers!

   c. You cut down on time in the kitchen. So grab a glass of wine and put your feet up!

   d. You'll have a stocked freezer full of healthy meals. It's like Christmas!

   e. I'm no dummy. All of these are advantages.

10. What is the ideal number of participants at a Freezer Cooking Party or in a Freezer Club?

    a. 12+ ("The more the merrier!")

    b. 8

    c. 6

    d. 2 ("I'm an introvert. Please let this be the right answer!")

That's it. Now turn the page to see how you did. (Cue the drumroll, please.)

ANSWERS

1. **c.** Like, forever! The USDA guidelines state, "Food stored constantly at 0°F will always be safe. Only the quality suffers with lengthy freezer storage." Pretty great, right? See the Freezer Storage Times chart on page 10 for freezing length recommendations.

2. **a.** Eggs in shell *and* **c.** Canned food. You can freeze almost any food *safely,* with the exception of these two. While mayonnaise does not freeze and thaw *well* (the texture gets funky), it *is* safe to freeze it. Tomatoes do fine in the freezer either raw or blanched first, but they are best used in soups, stews, or a sauce later. Go to page 5 to learn more about foods that do not freeze well.

3. **d.** None of the above!
   ▸ The USDA site says, "Freezing to 0°F inactivates any microbes—bacteria, yeasts, and molds—present in food. Once thawed, however, these microbes can again become active, multiplying under the right conditions to levels that can lead to foodborne illness." Basically, handle all frozen foods just as you would fresh food and cook them thoroughly. For a guide on the safe minimum internal temperatures various foods should reach during cooking, Google the term *USDA Safe Minimum Internal Temperature Chart.*

   ▸ There is little change in nutrient value during freezer storage. Score!

   ▸ If you think freezing food makes it yucky, we can't *wait* for you to try our recipes. Sorry to break it to you, but you've been misled. All of our recipes work as a fresh meal *or* after being frozen. Seriously.

4. **c.** 0°F. Many freezers are mistakenly kept too warm. Track the temperature in your freezer with an inexpensive refrigerator/freezer thermometer.

5. **True.** Sort of. This is a little tricky. While it is *safe* to freeze items in their original packaging, we wouldn't recommend it. That's because most of the time that kind of packaging is permeable to air, which can make your meat taste like lightly roasted cardboard. (Mmmm.) However, you *can* freeze unopened vacuum-sealed food. No air is getting in those bad boys.

6. **(1) In the refrigerator, (2) in cold water, and (3) in the microwave.** Read more about these three safe methods for defrosting foods on page 11.

7. **False.** Good news, right? If food is safely thawed in the refrigerator, it is safe to refreeze it without cooking. However, the texture and color may be compromised upon refreezing and thawing.

8. **d.** The rear center. Duh.

9. **e.** All of the above. Told you, I'm no dummy. Read about all the benefits of freezer cooking with friends on page 3.

10. **c.** 6. We've found that if you have more than six participants, it's "too many cooks in the kitchen." Fewer than six, and you'll have a hard time stocking your freezer.

WHAT YOUR SCORE TELLS YOU

Now, here's the fun part of any teen quiz. What does your score say about you as a Freezer Cooker (yes, we just made up that term)?

0 TO 3 CORRECT ANSWERS: *Newbie Freezer Cooker.* Hey, we've been in your shoes. Once upon a time we both thawed meals on the counter (a big no-no!) and let so much food go to waste not knowing it could be frozen. Don't sweat it. You're miles ahead of where we were because you have this book in hand. We've got your back!

4 TO 6 CORRECT ANSWERS: *Up-and-Coming Freezer Cooker.* You have some base knowledge to work from but room to grow. That's a great place to be in. Maybe you've tried freezer cooking by yourself, but we'll show you how to take it to a whole new level by sharing the load with friends.

7 TO 9 CORRECT ANSWERS: *Experienced Freezer Cooker.* Pat yourself on the back. This is a solid score! (Are you sure you didn't cheat, just a little?) Onward to freezer cooking and filling that freezer to the brim, oh experienced one!

10 CORRECT ANSWERS: *O.A.F.C. (Overachiever Freezer Cooker).* "We're not worthy! We're not worthy!" Seriously, you should have written this book. Henceforth, you shall be known as O.A.F.C.

Part I

MAKING FREEZER COOKING A LIFESTYLE

Congratulations on taking your first freezer cooking quiz ever! If you're like we once were, you noticed a few gaps in your freezer cooking knowledge. No prob. As self-proclaimed (and tongue-in-cheek!) "freezer cooking evangelists," we're passionate about resourcing you for this lifestyle change that will benefit you and your family over the long haul.

In this section, we'll quickly motivate and set you up for success before you dive into filling that cold chest, addressing questions like:

▸ What are the advantages of freezer cooking?

▸ How should you freeze and thaw meals?

▸ What foods should you avoid freezing?

▸ How long can you freeze foods?

▸ Do I need a deep freezer?

We'll also equip you with two ways to share the freezer stocking load with friends, both at one-time Freezer Cooking Parties and in an ongoing Freezer Club. Learning to freezer cook on our own and with friends has positively transformed how we prepare food, shop, eat, and spend our time and money. We think this lifestyle shift will do the same for you, too. Let's get started on a change you won't regret!

FREEZER COOKING PARTY: A *one-time event* where a group gathers together to cook, assemble, and package a variety of freezer meals.

FREEZER CLUB: An *ongoing* small group of friends who commit to regularly cooking freezer-friendly meals for one another. Members prepare recipes at home on their own time and then swap at a meeting.

a deep dive into the cold chest

Freezer cooking pays off over time, but there is a little bit of a learning curve. That's why, in this chapter, we're aiming to motivate you with the big picture of this lifestyle. Then, we'll walk you through six essential steps to making successful freezer meals, as well as address all your *burning* questions. From the very basics to the very specific, we are diving in and sharing everything we know.

WHAT ARE THE BENEFITS OF FREEZER COOKING?

As we mentioned in our own stories in the introduction, freezer cooking can help you and your family in so many ways. Wow, isn't it motivating to know that it provides all of the following benefits?

1. Saves money because you'll be buying in bulk and eating at home.

It's no secret that when you buy food in bulk quantities, it is usually cheaper. By planning your meals, especially in a Freezer Club (see page 25), and cooking in large quantities, you'll see your grocery bill go down significantly. We've found that when we cook this way, a four-serving meal tends to cost around $8 to $12 depending on the ingredients needed. This translates to about $2 to

$3 per person for a wholesome, healthy meal. Plus, having ready-to-go meals within reach reduces the temptation to spend cash eating out. Who needs to wait for takeout when you have Turkey Pesto Paninis or Parmesan and Herb Chicken Tenders in the freezer, just a few minutes away from being piping hot?

2. Cuts down on prep and cooking time, leaving you with more freedom to relax and spend time with loved ones.

Let's be honest. Cooking a well-rounded, healthy dinner every night is a daunting task for anyone. Deciding what to make, shopping, prepping, cooking, and cleaning up can sap the last bit of physical and mental energy you have after a long day. Add a few tired, grumpy kids to the mix, and the dinner hour can be quite a challenge. By having meals that you doubled from a previous meal or made with a group of friends (see Chapters 2 and 3) ready to go in the freezer, you'll cut down on all those extra little trips to the store during the week. Even more importantly, you'll reduce your prep, cooking, and cleanup time regularly, leaving weeknights freer to relax, spend time with your family, exercise, enjoy hobbies, or whatever else has been crowded out of your life by the daily cooking grind!

3. Provides a wide variety of wholesome, nutrient-dense meals to help you eat more healthfully.

Freezer cooking, especially using the recipes in this book, makes homemade food full of real, wholesome ingredients readily available. We believe eating a healthy diet means consuming a variety of whole foods, ones that are closest to their natural state. Through research and our own experience, we've learned that when we consume *real* food—with an emphasis on lots of produce, whole grains, organic or local meats and dairy, wild-caught seafood, and healthy fats—our bodies tend to do what they are supposed to do. We have more energy, sleep better, avoid headaches and stomachaches, and feel comfortably full and stop from overeating more easily. Whole foods are the fuel our bodies are made to run on.

The good news is that freezer cooking can help you eat more whole foods in two main ways. First, cooking from scratch allows you to control what goes into your food, thus avoiding loads of extra sodium, sugar, unhealthy fats, preservatives, additives, and food dyes that are packed into fast food and other processed, store-bought foods. Second, freezer cooking also means

you will have nutritious, easy-to-prepare meals at your fingertips all the time, which results in fewer fast-food runs or pre-packaged meal purchases. Once you learn how easy it is to stock your freezer, your family will be well on their way to eating a wide range of nutritious foods every day.

4. Allows you to always have meals on hand to take to a friend in need.

With freezer cooking, it's easy to have meals ready to go to take to new parents or others in need. Over the years, we have given many new moms, people in crisis, grandparents, college students, and even a man recently released from prison some extra freezer meals to bake or warm up at their convenience. With meals in the freezer, you can be that friend who shows up at someone's doorstep with a healthy dinner and a few words of encouragement. It's a simple act of caring and thoughtfulness that can make a bigger impact than you may realize.

If you choose to freezer cook with friends, there are even more advantages to reap.

5. Expands your family's palate.

It's easy to fall into a rut and make the same meals on a regular rotation, isn't it? A Freezer Cooking Party or Freezer Club allows you to experience different kinds of cuisines, flavors, and ingredients that you may not normally prepare at home. This has been a great palate-expanding experience for our children (and husbands!). Even better, it has also allowed us to get more nutritional variety into our bodies and the bodies of our families.

6. Helps you become a better cook.

Among other things, freezer cooking with friends can stretch you as a home cook. It has forced us to try our hand at all kinds of new recipes. As a result, our recipe repertoire and cooking skills have grown beyond anything we could have accomplished on our own. It's almost like taking a cooking class with your friends, but at the end you all leave as savvier, more experienced cooks with stocked freezers!

7. It's fun.

Last and certainly not least, we think freezer cooking with our friends is simply fun! At our Freezer Club meetings and Freezer Cooking Parties, we often have coffee, wine, snacks, and a great time hanging out together. To top it all off, you get to come home and fill your freezer to the brim with already-prepared healthy meals. It's the perfect night out, if you ask us!

WHAT ARE THE STEPS TO SUCCESSFULLY FREEZING MEALS?

Freezer cooking isn't especially hard, but there are a few keys to success. To get the tastiest results, keep these six simple steps in mind.

STEP 1
Use high-quality fresh ingredients that stand up well to freezing and thawing.

Rule #1 of freezer cooking is that what you put in is what you get out. Be sure to select only the freshest, high-quality foods to use in your freezer meals. If an ingredient didn't taste good to begin with, it certainly won't be better after freezing.

Also keep in mind that some foods freeze and thaw much better than others.

FOODS THAT TYPICALLY DON'T FREEZE AND THAW WELL

Note: Some of these ingredients will freeze well within a recipe. However, the texture may change if frozen as a single ingredient.

- ▶ **VEGETABLES:** celery, cucumbers, lettuce, onions, bell peppers, potatoes, radishes, sprouts
- ▶ **FRUITS:** apples, citrus fruits, grapes, melons

- ▶ **DAIRY:** soft cheeses, cottage cheese, cream cheese, cream, custard, mayonnaise, sour cream, yogurt
- ▶ **OTHER:** canned food still in cans, eggs in shells, fried foods, pasta cooked beyond al dente

While it's safe to freeze most foods, the texture and taste of some are extremely compromised after being frozen and thawed, as the box on page 5 shows. Additionally, seasoning and spices can tend to get stronger when they sit in the freezer in a meal. Season lightly before freezing, and add additional seasonings when reheating or serving.

STEP 2
Chill cooked dishes before freezing.

It's important to let freshly cooked dishes cool before placing them in the freezer. There are a number of reasons for this. First, putting foods that are still warm in the freezer can raise the freezer's temperature. This can cause surrounding frozen items to partially thaw and refreeze, which can alter the taste and texture of those

foods. Second, placing hot food in a plastic freezer bag or container can result in the plastic releasing chemicals into the food. Third, warm food freezes so slowly that ice crystals form on top, which can also alter the texture of the freezer meal.

To avoid contamination while allowing food to cool, never let perishable food sit out on the counter for longer than 2 hours. To bring down the temperature more quickly, place partially cooled food in a shallow, wide container and refrigerate it, uncovered, until cold. Or, to chill soup or stew quickly, pour it into a metal bowl and set it in a larger bowl filled halfway with ice water. Stir occasionally.

STEP 3
Freeze in an airtight, freezable container.

There are multiple ways that meals can be stored in the freezer. Your freezing method will likely depend on the space in your freezer, the types of meals you make, and what containers you have on hand.

Whatever method you choose, the goal is to prevent the food from being exposed to air, which can result in freezer burn. Freezer burn occurs when the moisture in the outer layers evaporates, leaving behind "dry" pockets. While it isn't harmful to eat freezer-burned food, the texture and flavor can be adversely affected. Wrapping food tightly and using the four freezing methods we recommend on page 8 will help keep freezer burn at bay.

It's also helpful to label your meals so you know exactly what they are and how long they have been in the freezer. Affix a label to each container with the name of the dish, number of servings (or volume/weight), and the date you put it in the freezer.

STEP 4

Freeze quickly and at the right temperature.

The faster food freezes, the better its quality will be once it's defrosted. Slowly frozen food forms large ice crystals that may turn the food mushy. Here are some tips for freezing food quickly and at the right temperature:

▸ Store all foods at 0°F or lower to retain vitamin content, flavor, texture, and color. Use a freezer thermometer to ensure this.

▸ Do not crowd the freezer, so that there is enough room for air to circulate around food, allowing it to freeze rapidly. Never stack packages to be frozen. Instead, spread them out in one layer on various shelves, stacking them only after they're frozen solid.

▸ Store soups and stews in freezer bags, which can be placed flat and will freeze quickly.

▸ Store foods in small servings, when possible, to help them freeze quickly. This also allows you to defrost only what you need.

A secondary freezer is not a necessity for freezer cooking, but it can be helpful if you want to make freezer cooking a lifestyle. It can actually store food at a more constant, lower temperature than a refrigerator's freezer, protecting the taste and texture of food longer. Plus, it provides room for stocking up on ingredients when they are on sale, saving produce when it is in season, and stacking up all of those freezer meals you'll be accumulating soon. A secondary freezer doesn't have to be huge and expensive, though. Simply start with a standard chest freezer. If you want something bigger, both of us have the Frigidaire Gallery 2-in-1 Upright Freezer and love it.

STEP 5

Follow recommended storage times for freezing meals.

From a safety standpoint, food that is properly packaged and safely frozen (kept at a constant temperature of 0°F or lower) can be frozen indefinitely. Yes, *indefinitely*! However, even though something may be safe to eat, that doesn't mean it will taste its best after a long time in the freezer.

The chart on page 10 provides some general guidelines for how long to freeze particular foods and still maintain their quality. These recommendations are conservative and somewhat subjective, to be honest. We have frozen food much longer than some of these times with good results. There are many variables that affect the amount of time food can be frozen (type of freezer, ingredients in the recipe, quality of the packaging, etc.), so it's hard to say exactly when a freezer meal will go "bad." Regardless, it is good to have a rough idea of how long something can hang out in your freezer.

STEP 6

Thaw frozen food properly.

Let's begin with the biggest no-no when it comes to thawing perishable foods: no thawing on the counter! Thawing at room

(CONTINUED ON PAGE 11)

THE FOUR BEST STORAGE METHODS FOR FREEZER FOOD

Based on our experience, we prefer the following four freezing methods for storing freezer food.

1. Rigid Containers

There are quite a few different types of rigid containers out there: glass, metal, foil, plastic, etc. Our preferred type is an oven- and freezer-safe glass baking dish with a lid. We like that they are reusable, safe, and sturdy. They also can go from freezing to thawing to baking. Our personal favorite glass freezer containers are Anchor Hocking glass baking dishes with the Truefit lid, which you'll find on the MightyNest Web site. Note: Do not take glass dishes directly from the freezer and place them in a hot oven, as they can shatter. Always read the manufacturer's instructions.

If you're not quite ready to invest in some glass dishes with lids, you can most likely find disposable baking dishes at your local grocery store. It's worth noting that we do not recommend using disposable aluminum pans with lids for long-term storage in the freezer. These pans can be helpful when making a frozen meal to give away to a friend or someone in need. However, it's important to keep in mind that some highly acidic or alkaline foods, like tomato sauce, citrus, vinegar, some vegetables, egg yolks, and even salty foods, can react with aluminum, changing flavors or causing discoloration.

2. Freezer Storage Bags

Freezer storage bags are quite useful and safe when it comes to freezing, as long as you don't heat them up or place hot foods in them. This can cause chemicals from the plastic to leach into your food. While freezer storage bags may not be an option for every recipe, they can be a great alternative to a rigid container. They work well for marinades, soups, and baked goods and, if frozen flat, can be a space saver in the freezer.

3. Plastic Wrap and Aluminum Foil

When it comes to recipes that can be portioned out individually (like burritos, paninis, wraps, etc.), wrapping them first in plastic wrap and then in foil is a helpful option, making it possible to thaw one at a time. This method also works best for wrapping and freezing pizzas. Plastic wrap and foil allow you to utilize a rigid container that doesn't have a lid. Simply cover tightly in a few layers of plastic wrap, then one or two layers of foil, and squeeze out any excess air before placing in the freezer.

4. Mason Jars

Freezing food in Mason jars (not just glass jars, but Mason jars that are made for canning) is often overlooked but can prove to be quite useful. As long as you use a wide-mouthed jar (one without shoulders) and don't go over the "freeze-fill" line that is found on Mason jars, most things can be frozen in them without a problem. It's essential to leave room at the top of the jar because liquids will expand when frozen. Not only are these jars excellent for freezing soups, marinara sauce, pesto, chicken stock, or other liquid recipes, but they can also work for storing herbs, citrus zest, or bread crumbs.

FREEZER STORAGE TIMES

Recommended storage times are for quality purposes only, since frozen foods remain safe indefinitely.

Fresh Meats

Steaks = 6 to 12 months

Chops = 6 months

Roasts = 4 to 12 months

Chicken or turkey, whole = 1 year

Chicken or turkey, parts = 9 months

Meats

Bacon, raw = 1 month

Sausage, raw = 1 to 2 months

All cooked meat = 2 to 3 months

Uncooked ground beef or pork = 3 to 4 months

Lunch meats, unopened = 1 to 2 months

Soups and stews = 2 to 3 months

Uncooked ground chicken or turkey = 3 to 4 months

Cooked chicken covered in a sauce, broth, or marinade = 6 months

Fish and Shellfish

Fish, cooked = 4 to 6 months

Shellfish, cooked = 3 months

Fresh shrimp and scallops = 3 to 6 months

Raw fish, lean = 6 months

Raw fish, fatty = 2 to 3 months

Fruits and Vegetables

Most fruits and vegetables (except those mentioned in the chart on page 5) = 8 to 12 months

Bananas = 3 months

Artichokes, eggplant = 6 to 8 months

Asparagus = 8 to 10 months

Tomatoes (overripe or sliced) = 2 months

Baked Goods

Bread = 6 months

Muffins and scones = 3 months

Quick breads = 3 months

Cookies = 6 months

Pancakes and waffles = 1 to 2 months

Bagels = 3 months

Casseroles

Assembled and uncooked = 3 to 4 months

Previously cooked = 2 to 3 months

Other

Pesto = 1 to 2 months

Chicken broth = 4 to 6 months

Bread crumbs = 6 months

Shredded cheese = 6 months

Marinara sauce = 4 to 6 months

Butter = 6 to 9 months

Cookie dough = 2 months

temperature puts foods with meat, eggs, and dairy products in them within the danger zone, a temperature range where harmful bacteria grow at a rapid pace. Maybe you've thawed something on the counter before and didn't have any problems. But, the truth of the matter is, it's not worth the risk of possible food poisoning. The good news is that there are three safe ways to defrost your food, outlined below.

ARMED AND READY

Now that you've taken a deep dive with us into the cold chest, it's time to discuss how to make freezer cooking a sustainable part of your life. You can start cooking through our recipe collection on your own, doubling and freezing meals as you go. Or, we have a fun and practical suggestion for you: Start freezer cooking with friends!

THE THREE SAFE WAYS TO THAW FROZEN FOOD

1. Thaw in the refrigerator.

The most effective and safest way to thaw a freezer meal is to put it in the refrigerator for 24 to 48 hours. The exact thawing time will depend on the size of the meal. Make sure to place it on a plate to catch any condensation or leaks as it thaws.

It's worth noting that once you have safely thawed your raw or cooked frozen food in the refrigerator, you can still refreeze it if it's been stored at 40°F or lower. Just keep in mind that there may be a loss of quality due to the moisture lost through thawing.

This method works best when you develop a menu plan at the beginning of the week and then move the freezer meals to the refrigerator a few days ahead of time. But we realize that great planning doesn't always happen. So there are two faster thawing methods you can use.

2. Thaw in cold water.

Another safe thawing option is to place the food in a leak-proof plastic bag and immerse it in cold water, changing the water every 30 minutes. This still takes a bit of time, but it's quicker than the refrigerator option. According to the USDA, "Small packages of meat, poultry, or seafood—about a pound—may thaw in an hour or less. A 3- to 4-pound package may take 2 to 3 hours. For whole turkeys, estimate about 30 minutes per pound." After using this method of thawing, cook your food immediately.

3. Thaw in the microwave.

The fastest option is to microwave-defrost food in a microwave-safe dish, according to your microwave's instructions. The reason this is the last option (our least favorite) is because this method can tend to dry out food a bit. Regardless, sometimes you just need to quickly thaw something, so the microwave it is! Make sure to cook your food immediately after using this method as well.

throw a freezer cooking party

It was Friday night, and five friends were on their way to my (Polly's) house for a Freezer Cooking Party. While we were all in different stages of life, we had one thing in common: We were busy moms who wanted to feed our families healthy meals. In this season of life, a girls' night is always a fun event to look forward to. But a girls' night *with a purpose* is even more alluring. We weren't only coming together to chat about life, catch up on family news, or share (and vent about) parenting successes and failures, we were also preparing dinners for weeks to come!

WHAT EXACTLY IS A FREEZER COOKING PARTY?

A Freezer Cooking Party is a designated time when a group gathers together to cook, assemble, and package a variety of meals that can be taken home, frozen, and later gobbled up on busy mornings or nights. From expectant moms, to time-crunched single people, to couples without kids, we've found that almost everyone breathes a sigh of relief after stocking their freezer with a variety of healthy, delicious meals.

A Freezer Cooking Party is also a great environment to learn about and try out freezer cooking for the first time. The setup is conducive to the freezer cooking veteran or newbie. The fact that it is a one-time event makes it appealing to those who aren't sure they want to jump into an ongoing Freezer Club (see Chapter 3) just yet. However, if you like the party, then setting up a club may be a great next step for you and your friends.

HOW TO THROW A FREEZER COOKING PARTY

Ready to plan your own Freezer Cooking Party with your friends? Great! Yes, there is a bit of organizing and work to do in order to set one up, but you'll find that it can be done fairly quickly and easily. We've broken the party-planning process down into three simple steps:

1. Organize the Party
2. Prepare for the Party
3. Host the Party

Let's jump in and get you and your friends on your way to filling those freezers!

STEP 1
Organize the Party

1. PICK A DATE AND TIME

As the host, you have the luxury of setting the time and date for the party. I've primarily hosted my parties on weekends. Since it's also a fun evening with friends, most people don't mind giving up a Friday or Saturday night to accomplish the task. Saturday afternoons have worked well, too. Just keep in mind that the party will likely take 2 to 4 hours, depending on how much preparation is done beforehand and how many meals you'll prepare.

2. ESTABLISH A LOCATION

Depending on how many people you invite, you will need a somewhat large kitchen to host the party. My average-to-small-size kitchen works fine for four or five people, but if you have more than that, I'd recommend reaching out to the people you invite to see if anyone has a bigger space that they would be willing to open up for the party. A kitchen with plenty of counter space or tables that can be used to assemble meals is ideal. Keep in mind that you will likely do some food preparation at the party (brown meat, cook rice, etc.), so you will need a space with adequate kitchen supplies and appliances.

3. INVITE YOUR FRIENDS

Now that you have a date, time, and location picked, you can start inviting your crew. I'd recommend aiming to have around six people at your party. This will allow you to prepare a variety of meals. With more than six friends, though, it can get a bit crowded and expensive. If six is an intimidating number, you can always begin with a smaller group.

I find it's helpful to send out two different e-mails to the participants in advance. The first one will explain the concept and serve as the invitation. The second one will assign a meal to each participant, provide any additional details, and serve as a reminder for the event.

When crafting your first e-mail (sample at right), keep it simple and fun, but make sure you provide enough background information so that people know what to expect. In your own words, this e-mail should include the following information:

▶ Concept of a Freezer Cooking Party

▶ Why you want to host one

▶ Date and time (and location if you know it)

▶ Request an RSVP.

▶ If it applies, you may want to mention that this is an adults' night out, and they will need to arrange childcare.

▶ Assure them you will send more details once you know who will be attending.

Once you have firm RSVPs from your invitees, you can start to figure out more details, like what recipes you will be using.

SAMPLE E-MAIL #1: INVITATION TO THE PARTY

Here is an example of what an initial e-mail could look like to a group of friends who have never attended a freezer meal party.

. . . .

Hey Friends!

Hope everyone is loving this fall weather as much as we are. I can't get enough of it.

I'm really excited to tell you about something that I think will benefit ALL of us. I don't know about you, but dinnertime around my house is crazy. It's hard for me to cook when the kids are cranky, it's witching hour for the baby, and I'm just plain tired. This is why I'm excited to host a Freezer Cooking Party. I wanted to see if you'd join me! I'm hoping it will feel like a girls' night out but with a purpose—assembling freezer meals. I think it will not only save us cooking time at home but also a good amount of money.

If you haven't heard of a Freezer Cooking Party, allow me to explain. In short, each of us will:

✓ Be assigned one recipe.

✓ Bring enough ingredients of that assigned recipe to make six meals.

✓ Assemble the meals at my place.

✓ Go home with six different meals that are all freezer-friendly.

Here are the details:

When: Friday, September 30, 6:00 p.m.

Where: My house (1234 Main Street)

Cost: Depending on what recipes we decide on, my best guess is it will end up costing about $8 to $10 for a four-serving meal. If six people attend, that will end up being around $48 to $60 a person for six meals, or only $2 to $2.50 per serving.

RSVP: If you could, let me know if you want to join the party. Like I said, I want to round up about six people, so please let me know either way.

Note: Please arrange your own childcare, if it applies.

If you have any dietary restrictions or family members with allergies, now is the time to let me know. We will do our best to create our menu plan around your needs. I'll also be sure to run the recipe ideas past you to make sure they will be okay.

Once I have our team of six recruited, I will send out another e-mail with more details, including what recipes we will make, what exactly to bring, and any other important information.

I hope you can join us!

Polly

4. SELECT RECIPES FOR THE PARTY

Next, you'll have the task of choosing recipes for your party. From experience, we know that selecting recipes for a Freezer Cooking Party can be daunting. It can be hard to find family-friendly, easy-to-assemble-in-bulk, freezer-friendly meals that aren't packed with additives and preservatives. Do not fret, my friends. We have paved the way and done the hard work for you.

On page 18 you will find a collection of menu plans. Each plan includes a variety of tried-and-true recipes that complement each other well. You also have the freedom to swap out a meal or two if another recipe sounds irresistible or if you want to include one that isn't in this book.

STEP 2
Prepare for the Party

Before the event, you'll want to make sure to complete these steps:

1. SEND A CONFIRMATION E-MAIL

Preferably 1 to 2 weeks before the party (in order to give friends time to shop and prepare), send out an e-mail with the following information:

▶ Confirmed date, time, and location of the party.

▶ Each person's assigned recipe and, if you want to, directions for how to scale it up for the size of the group (see specific instructions in "How to Scale Up Recipes to Cook in Bulk" on page 19).

▶ Ask guests to look at their recipe and, if possible, to prepare some ingredients ahead of time (i.e., brown ground beef,

cook rice, chop and/or cook chicken, cook bacon, etc.). These small things cut down assembly time later.

▶ Remind guests to bring the following:

✓ **Freezer containers.** As the host, it is your job to look at the recipes and decide which containers will work best to transport each meal. Communicate this information to your participants so they know what to bring!

✓ **A cooler to transport food home.** You'd be surprised how hard it is to juggle six meals to and from your car. Nobody wants spilled jambalaya on their car floor, either!

✓ **Receipts and cash.** If you are concerned about everyone paying the same amount for each meal, tell participants to bring their receipts and small bills in order to settle up if there was a major discrepancy in spending.

✓ **Any cooking utensils that their recipe might require.** Encourage participants to look over their recipe, think through what utensils they may need, and either bring them to the party or double-check with their host to make sure they will be available.

2. MAKE HARD COPIES OF EACH RECIPE FOR EVERYONE

This simple step *really* helps the assembly process. It's so much easier to follow directions that are right in front of you rather than trying to share a cookbook or looking at them online. Additionally, each

SAMPLE E-MAIL #2: CONFIRM THE PARTY DETAILS

Here is a sample of what your confirmation e-mail may sound like:

. . . .

Hey Freezer Cooking Party Friends!

I'm so excited about our Freezer Cooking Party in 2 weeks. Just as a reminder, our party will be at my house at 6:00 p.m. on Friday, the 30th. Below are some of the details that you will need to know before coming.

I've assigned each of you a freezer-friendly recipe that I pulled from this fabulous cookbook, *From Freezer to Table*. Please bring enough ingredients for that recipe to make 24 servings, or the equivalent of six freezer meals. I'd recommend buying ingredients in bulk or trying to find sales to save money.

Here are the recipes:

Leslie: Apple Raisin Baked French Toast

Kathy: Janny's Roasted Chicken

Emily: Family Favorite Baked Meatballs

Rachel: Turkey Pesto Paninis

Lynn: Straight from Alaska Salmon Burgers

Polly: Killer Carnitas

I'm attaching copies of each recipe to this e-mail so you can see what is in yours.

When looking at your recipe instructions, ask yourself if there is anything you could do in advance to prepare it. This will save us a lot of time (and mess) when we get together. Also, be sure to bring any extra cooking utensils you may need. I'm not sure if I will have enough cutting boards, baking sheets, etc.

As I look at our recipes, I think the best way to get these home safely to your freezer is to bring two 13" x 9" rigid containers and four gallon-size plastic freezer bags. I'd also recommend bringing a large cooler to make it easier to transport your meals home. No one wants spilled food in their car!

Bring your receipts and some small bills. That way, if one person spent a lot more, we can even it up.

Please let me know if you have any questions at all.

Polly

FREEZER MEAL PARTY PLANS

Party Plan 1
- Apple Maple Sausage Bites *(page 56)*
- Janny's Roasted Chicken *(page 79)*
- Family Favorite Baked Meatballs *(page 96)*
- Turkey Pesto Paninis *(page 129)*
- Straight from Alaska Salmon Burgers *(page 132)*
- Killer Carnitas *(page 196)*

Party Plan 2
- Hash Brown Breakfast Bake *(page 49)*
- Cilantro Lime Chicken *(page 68)*
- Chili-Rubbed Beef Brisket *(page 195)*
- Foolproof Roasted Pork Tenderloin *(page 114)*
- Not So Fishy Sticks *(page 134)*
- French Dip Sandwiches *(page 198)*

Party Plan 3
- Peaches and Cream Baked Oatmeal *(page 51)*
- Cheddar Chive Burgers *(page 98)*
- Chicken and Broccoli Foil Packs *(page 75)*
- Sweet and Savory Pork Chops *(page 118)*
- Zesty Marinated Shrimp *(page 137)*
- Chicken Parmesan Sliders *(page 205)*

Party Plan 4
- Apple Raisin Baked French Toast *(page 57)*
- Grilled Honey Dijon Chicken Sandwiches *(page 80)*
- Polly's Signature Taco Soup *(page 209)*
- Four-Ingredient Seasoned Pork Chops *(page 116)*
- Yum Loaves *(page 115)*
- Curt's Slow Cooker Jambalaya *(page 203)*

Party Plan 5
- Cinnamon Oatmeal Pancakes *(page 54)*
- Sheet Pan Lemon-Garlic Chicken and Veggies *(page 88)*
- Mini Turkey and Veggie Cheeseburgers *(page 127)*
- English Muffin Pizzas *(page 160)*
- Ham and Swiss Glazed Paninis *(page 120)*
- Creamy Tomato Penne with Shrimp *(page 156)*

Party Plan 6 (Gluten-Free)
- Hash Brown Breakfast Bake *(page 49)*
- Janny's Roasted Chicken *(page 79)*
- Foolproof Roasted Pork Tenderloin *(page 114)*
- Polly's Signature Taco Soup *(page 209)*
- Zesty Marinated Shrimp *(page 137)*
- Cheddar Chive Burgers *(page 98)*

HOW TO SCALE UP RECIPES TO COOK IN BULK

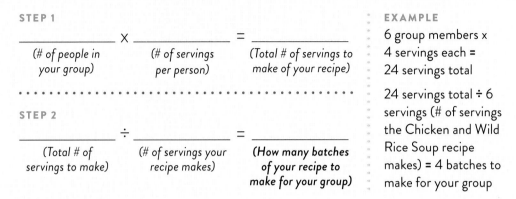

STEP 1

_____ X _____ = _____
(# of people in   (# of servings   (Total # of servings to
your group)   per person)   make of your recipe)

STEP 2

_____ ÷ _____ = _____
(Total # of   (# of servings your **(How many batches
servings to make)   recipe makes)   of your recipe to
                                          make for your group)**

EXAMPLE

6 group members x 4 servings each = 24 servings total

24 servings total ÷ 6 servings (# of servings the Chicken and Wild Rice Soup recipe makes) = 4 batches to make for your group

---

participant can take home a hard copy of each recipe to have for future reference.

3. HIT THE GROCERY STORE

Not only will you need to get ingredients for the recipe that you are assigned to make, but as the host, you might also consider getting a few drinks and snacks for your participants to munch on during the party. Having these available adds a fun "party" feel to the gathering.

STEP 3
Host the Party

The day of your Freezer Cooking Party has come. Now what? Here are a few suggestions to make the party go a bit more smoothly.

1. SET UP WORK STATIONS

Make a tentative plan about where each recipe will be assembled. If six people are attending, we have found it's easiest to create three work stations and team up everyone with a partner. Each team will make two recipes at their station. Think through if someone will need the stove, oven, or require use of the sink. Does a recipe need a lot of counter space, or can it be assembled in a small spot? Pull out any utensils that may be needed (if you have them) and place them at their designated work station. Lastly, provide a hard copy of each recipe at its station and a pen, in case the cook wants to make any notes along the way. Having a plan in place will allow you to direct your friends to the right spot as soon as they arrive with their ingredients.

2. SET UP SNACKS

Arrange a few snacks and drinks for everyone to enjoy as they arrive and throughout the party. Finger foods such as veggies and dip, cheese and crackers, and cookies work well. Drink options like wine, beer, coffee, and lemonade also add to the festive atmosphere. We've even been known to make mimosas at a midafternoon party, so feel free to get creative for your crowd.

3. ASSEMBLE THE MEALS

Once everyone has arrived and food stations are set up, assign participants to their work station and encourage them to get started. I like to start with a short powwow to explain what they will be doing, what recipes they will be making, what to do with their completed meals, and any other specific instructions they may need to know.

You'll find that some recipes will assemble quickly, while others will take a bit more time. If some friends get finished before others, encourage them to jump in and help at another station. Or they can start tackling the dirty dishes!

4. PROVIDE FREEZER MEAL LABELS

Once the freezer meals start to stack up, it can be hard to remember which is which, let alone the cooking or reheating instructions for each meal. To keep things organized, make sure to provide some type of label to document what the recipe is, when it was made, and how to thaw and cook it.

On our Web site, thrivinghomeblog.com, we provide some custom-made, printable freezer meal labels that you can purchase, download, and reprint as many times as you want. We have found these trendy labels to be critical in keeping meals organized. They also are perfect if you plan to give a meal away to a friend who couldn't be at the party or who needs some extra help.

TIME TO PARTY!

Hopefully you now have the confidence boost and knowledge you need to throw your own Freezer Cooking Party. If you find yourself wanting to do these regularly, you might consider starting your own Freezer Club. Learn more about how to do that in the next chapter!

FREEZER PARTY CHECKLIST

3 to 4 weeks in advance:

___ Pick date and time.

___ Establish location.

___ Send e-mail invite or query e-mail.

1 to 2 weeks in advance:

___ Select recipes.

___ Send confirmation e-mail with recipes and party details.

___ Buy drinks and snacks.

Day of the party:

___ Print off hard copies of recipes.

___ Print off freezer meal labels.

___ Set up work stations.

___ Set out drinks and snacks.

CHAPTER 3

start a
freezer club

Long before the Internet's obsession with freezer cooking, a small band of six friends, some with nursing infants in tow, eagerly pushed together a few coffee shop tables and sipped lattes. We laughed and chatted about life and then got down to business, discussing freezable recipes and planning our monthly menu. Even though our meeting served a utilitarian purpose, it was also a coveted evening out with friends while husbands put kids to bed.

This gathering in April 2007 was the start of my (Rachel's) Freezer Club, launching a 7-year-long stretch in which we would convene every 4 to 5 weeks, plan a menu together, and then swap meals we had made on our own time the previous month. Our Freezer Club provided healthy meals, accountability, and much-needed community during those physically draining "little years" of staying home with my young kids. It also taught me so much that still benefits our family today. My hope is that in this chapter you will learn from my group's triumphs and failures, and maybe be inspired and equipped to start your own Freezer Club.

WHAT IS A FREEZER CLUB, AND HOW IS IT DIFFERENT FROM A FREEZER COOKING PARTY?

A Freezer Club, which is perhaps the best option to make freezer cooking a lifestyle, is an *ongoing* small group of friends who commit to cooking freezer-friendly meals for one another every month or so. The members cook meals at home on their own time and then swap them at a meeting. A Freezer Cooking Party, on the other hand, is a *one-time event* where participants cook meals together in one kitchen for one another. It's a great place to try out freezer cooking with friends before diving into the regular commitment of a Freezer Club.

HOW DOES A FREEZER CLUB WORK?

A freezer club's structure works well because it allows the flexibility to shop and cook on your own time, yet provides a deadline for the meals. Here's how ours worked:

MONTHLY MEETING:
Assign next round's recipes and swap meals from previous round

COOK assigned recipes for the group at home

LABEL and **FREEZE** completed meals

SHARE recipes and cooking notes electronically with the group

STEP 1
Monthly Meeting

Since monthly meetings will look different group by group, I'm going to share what it looked like when *my* group would meet together. Our Freezer Club, which usually consisted of six women—although your club can include both genders, of course—met every month or so either at a coffee shop or one of our homes. One person kept the meeting moving and took notes. We rotated this responsibility so that the same person didn't shoulder the burden every time.

Of course, we'd start the meeting with some fun drinks and snacks! Then we would dive into evaluating the previous month's meals. We'd ask questions like, "Are there changes to the recipes to make them better next time?" and "Which ones would we like to eat again?" To make this a little easier, we passed around a sheet that listed all the meals and then checked "yes" if we wanted to have it again. Another option is setting up an anonymous form online where members can vote either for or against having each recipe again. The recipes that got the most votes became known as our Home Run Recipes.

Next, we'd plan our upcoming monthly menu. Each member brought three to five recipe ideas, and then our group voted for the top ones we preferred. We tried to make sure there was variety in the menu plan, including some beef, chicken, pasta, seafood, soup, breakfast, and vegetarian. Once we had our favorite recipes narrowed down, each person would choose two that she would make for everyone in the group. Polly's group makes only one meal per month, and that's where we suggest a new group to start. (Note: Read more about how many members to include and how many recipes to make per round below.)

At the end of the meeting, we got out our big coolers and began swapping freezer meals from the previous month's round of cooking. It felt like Christmas!

STEP 2
Cook at Home

Between meetings, members will cook assigned recipes on their own time. Depending on the needs of your group, you can decide how many servings per meal makes sense. Our group decided to make four-serving meals as the standard.

SAMPLE: MONTHLY FREEZER CLUB MENU

- ▶ Beef and Bean Burritos *(Rachel)*
- ▶ Baked Pink Pasta with Sausage *(Darcie)*
- ▶ Zesty Marinated Shrimp *(Carla)*
- ▶ Foolproof Roasted Pork Tenderloin *(Kelley)*
- ▶ Crispy Chicken with Lemony Butter Sauce *(Jen)*
- ▶ French Dip Sandwiches *(Devin)*

EMPIRE

tomato
bisque
8/26

marinara
8/26

Depending on the recipe, cooking enough food for six families takes about 1 to 3 hours from start to cleanup.

STEP 3
Label and Freeze Meals

You want to make sure group members know how to prepare your meal when they are ready to use it. So be sure to label the meals before freezing them, including the name, date prepared, who prepared it (in case a member has a question), and cooking instructions. For example, "Thaw. Bake at 350°F for 20 minutes" or "Thaw. Warm on low on the stove." You'll find freezer meal instructions at the bottom of all of our recipes.

STEP 4
Keep Track of New Recipes

I highly recommend creating an online database or hard-copy binder of recipes as you go. Before the meetings, each member can upload any new recipes to a shared online Freezer Meal folder or make copies to bring to the meeting. That way all the members can access and make any notes on the recipes. This will be an awesome index that you will use over and over!

STEP 5
Transport Meals

It's important to keep meals frozen until right before the meeting. Then, transport the food in a large cooler, so it remains frozen in transit and during the evening together.

QUESTIONS TO ASK BEFORE STARTING A FREEZER CLUB

Are you ready to start a Freezer Club? Intrigued at least? Then you will need to ask some key questions before starting so you can avoid potential pitfalls. One of the most important lessons I learned from my Freezer Club experience is this: **Communicate expectations from the beginning.** It will save you several headaches along the way and make things run more smoothly.

What is the ideal number of participants?

Freezer Clubs can have varying numbers of members. If you have a motivated group of home cooks and a member who can help administrate the group, I would say six members is an ideal number. That way if everyone cooks one recipe and you swap once a month, you'll be provided with six meals for each family per month. This means you'll have one or two freezer meals per week. Or if your group feels ambitious, you may decide to each make two meals, providing each person with 12 per month.

There was a season that I did a Freezer Club with just two of my friends as our families grew. We swapped one or two meals each month. This required less administration and time and still gave me a break from cooking a few times a month. The beauty of a Freezer Club is that you can shape it to serve the needs of your group members.

What are our Freezer Club values?

One thing you will quickly realize is that each group member will have different values when it comes to the recipes they prefer. Some will want to make the cheapest meals possible. Others may want to use local and organic ingredients. Some may want mostly kid-friendly (i.e., plain) foods, while others may want to branch out and try "interesting" recipes. And still others will need to work around food allergies or aversions.

It's essential to have an up-front discussion to establish and know your group's values from the very beginning. This will help everyone hone in on the kind of recipes to bring and how to budget, shop, and cook. If you are on the same page from the beginning, your Freezer Club will be off to a great start!

How often will we swap meals?

Decide at the beginning how often you want to meet and swap meals. Every 4 weeks? Every 6 weeks? It can change during busier seasons of life, too.

HOW DOES A FREEZER CLUB WORK?

It's pretty simple: Each member makes 6 batches of 1 recipe. When you meet together, everyone exchanges what they made, and you come home with 6 different meals!

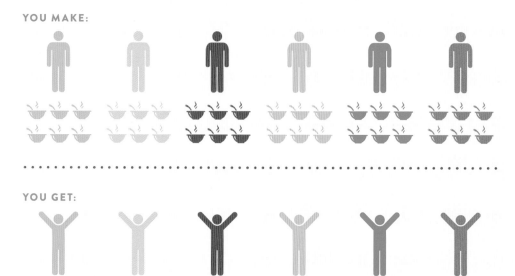

YOU MAKE:

YOU GET:

How many meals will we make each round?

Note that your group can cook one, two, or even more meals for each family in the Freezer Club each round. Polly's group cooks just one meal for all six families each round. We think this is a great starting point for most groups. Our members typically cooked two meals each round and found that was about right for us. Keep in mind that, depending on which recipes you choose, it will take you 1 to 3 hours to prepare and clean up one meal for six families. Do what is best for you and your life phase. Any extra freezer meals are helpful!

How many servings should each meal be?

The number of servings per freezer meal will really depend on the needs of your group. Our group always made a generous four servings for each family, since the majority of recipes make four to eight servings. But, if your group consists of singles or larger families, feel free to adjust the serving size requirements.

Our group created some "Freezer Club Guidelines and Reminders" in a shared online folder with portion guidelines for certain kinds of meals. Doing this in your club isn't necessary, but it may be helpful to think through at some point. For example, we agreed that burger meals would contain four $\frac{1}{4}$-pound burgers, chicken meals would be $1\frac{1}{2}$ pounds of meat, tilapia should include six fillets, and so on. We did this because recipes often vary when it comes to what a portion size actually is. When in doubt,

though, we tried to be generous with portions to avoid any hard feelings.

What containers will we use to swap freezer meals?

What containers to freeze meals in is another conversation your group will need to have up front when discussing values. You have a few options here and can turn back to Chapter 1 to read more about each of these types.

▶ **8" x 8" freezable glass dishes.** It might make sense for group members to all invest in the same number and kind of quality, safe, freezable glass dishes with lids. Polly and I personally use and recommend Anchor Hocking's Square Glass Cake Pan with Truefit Lid, which can be purchased at MightyNest. Then, these can be exchanged at each meeting so you always have the same number of dishes in your home. The advantage is that you can safely freeze *and* bake in these again and again. They also stack nicely in the freezer. The lid stands up to repeated freezing and dishwashing, unlike other brands we've tried, although do be aware that they aren't entirely leak-proof. In retrospect, I wish we had purchased these when we first started our group, although it can be a significant investment. One idea is to have everyone invest in a small number of these dishes to begin and use freezer bags for the rest of the meals.

▶ **BPA-free, gallon-size freezer bags.** These work well for some frozen foods, like meat in marinades, burritos, baked

goods, and even soups. However, they do not work for casseroles. *Important note:* Be sure to let your foods cool *completely* before putting them in plastic containers to avoid chemicals possibly being released into your food.

▶ **Reusable, BPA-free, freezer-safe plastic containers.** New and improved freezable plastic containers are always coming on the market. Search for ones that are big enough to hold a four-serving meal, are stackable, seal tightly, are BPA-free, and are freezer-safe. Do not microwave or bake food in these plastic containers, despite what they may advertise. Heating food in plastic can cause chemicals to leach into food. Always cool food completely before putting it in plastic containers. The downside to these containers is that they may last for only a few rounds of Freezer Club before cracking.

As we mentioned in Chapter 1, we do not recommend using disposable aluminum pans with lids for long-term storage in the freezer. Some highly acidic foods can react with aluminum, changing their flavors or causing discoloration.

How will we share the cost?

Every group is different when it comes to figuring out meal cost, but it's an important topic to discuss together at the beginning. Here are a few options to consider:

1. Everyone polices themselves. This is how our group operated. So, if I did a more expensive meal one month, I would plan to do a cheaper meal the next. As a group, we tried to rotate who did the salmon and steak meals, for instance, since they were usually more expensive. This option also allows people who are thrifty shoppers to use their talent and not feel constrained by meeting a minimum cost.

2. Set a cost range for members to shoot for each month. We found that most of our meals were about $8 to $12 at the time, since we used local and organic ingredients. This wasn't a hard-and-fast law for us, but it was a helpful rule of thumb.

3. Have everyone bring their grocery store receipts, tally up the group cost at your meeting, and divide out equally. The upside is that cost is always even for everyone. The downside is that it takes *a lot* of work, and someone will inevitably forget their receipts or lose them. There's also the occasional complication of people who purchase a side of beef for the freezer or those who grow some of their own ingredients, for instance. Figuring out exact cost can become tedious. We never attempted this route ourselves.

How will we evaluate meals?

Our group determined early on to be really open to feedback each month. This is the only way to get better at what you're doing and determine which meals are the very best freezer meals. To evaluate, we decided to vote at each meeting on a sheet that was passed around listing the previous month's meals. We would simply check a box if we wanted a meal again or not. We also sometimes offered one another suggestions to make a meal work better next time, if we thought it had potential.

Another option that might work well is creating an online form to vote. This would be more anonymous, thus allowing people to be more honest with their feedback. While you could skip evaluating, the advantage is that you can remake the successful ones again and again.

Who will be the administrator?

The larger your group is, the more helpful it is to have one person be the administrator. This person will keep track of who is making what meal, keep the meeting moving along, send out e-mail reminders, etc. You can even rotate who does this every few months, so everyone has a turn.

What about picky eaters?

There is unfortunately no way to please every single person. But by bringing our

---

FREEZER CLUB MONTHLY CHECKLIST

Before the Meeting

___ Review previously assigned recipes, develop shopping list, and buy in bulk.

___ Plan ahead which days you'll cook your Freezer Club meals during the month (so you aren't stressed at the last minute). Allow about 1 to 3 hours of prep and cleanup time per meal.

___ Label meals with the recipe name, your initials, date, and cooking instructions. Freeze.

___ Share new recipes and any cooking notes with the group (either online or make hard copies).

___ Collect three to five recipe ideas to share at the upcoming meeting.

At the Meeting

___ Evaluate: Vote on which recipes from the previous round your family would like to have again. Add any helpful suggestions for next time, if needed.

___ Share recipes and decide together on the freezer meal menu for the next round.

___ Decide the date of the next meeting.

___ Swap meals from the previous round . . . and fill your freezer!

own recipe suggestions, trying our best to please most members, and creating a menu full of variety, our families were usually pleased with the menu each month. Plus, one of the advantages to Freezer Club is that it exposed our families to new foods and really stretched my kids' palates. They were often more open to trying a meal from "Ms. Darcie" than from me!

If there was a meal I knew no one in our family would eat, then sometimes I would swap with another member who loved that one. She would receive two of those meals, and I would get two of the same meal we loved.

READY TO TAKE FREEZER COOKING WITH FRIENDS TO THE NEXT LEVEL?

The way I cooked and shopped never looked the same after I learned how to use my freezer in an ongoing Freezer Club. I hope you can have fun with friends, fill your freezer, and learn together with your own Freezer Club very soon!

Part II

75+
WHOLE
FOOD
FREEZER
MEALS

Time to get cooking! As you work through our index of delicious, wholesome, freezer-friendly, and easy-to-prepare recipes on your own or with a community of friends, our hope is that your home life experiences real change. Stocking your freezer is merely a means to an end. And that glorious end is gathering around the table and connecting with your loved ones over good food.

When it comes to our recipes, we consider ourselves "real food realists" rather than "whole food purists." We strive to balance making healthy food, managing our limited time, and creating meals our family will love. So, as you scan through our ingredients, you may notice that we use shortcuts from the store occasionally. (Who has time to make hand-rolled tortillas or ferment their own soy sauce?) This moderate take on a whole foods diet has enabled us to make it a sustainable lifestyle over the years. We encourage you to always take the time to read the labels of store-bought ingredients, scanning for the ones with the most recognizable and fewest ingredients. Oftentimes, you'll find the best products in the health food section.

Cooking oil is an essential part of many of our recipes. We sometimes offer the option of using either olive oil or avocado oil. Both are minimally processed, healthy oils. Olive oil is a staple in most pantries, which is why we offer it as an option. However, avocado oil works wonderfully for high-heat cooking and baking. That's because it is tasteless and has a higher smoke point (the point at which an oil breaks down) than olive oil, making it a safer and more versatile option. You can find avocado oil in most grocery store chains now at an increasingly affordable price.

Lastly, we want to reiterate that all of our recipes can be made as a fresh meal and/or turned into a freezer meal by using the simple Freezer Meal Instructions at the bottom of each one. Gotta love recipe versatility! Now, let's get cooking, freezing, and eating well at home!

Apple Raisin Baked
French Toast, *page 57*

EASY MINI EGG CASSEROLES

It's no surprise that this is one of the most popular recipes on our blog, Thriving Home. These mini casseroles can be made from basic ingredients you likely have on hand and provide a protein-rich breakfast that stays with you all morning. Feel free to up the nutrition ante by adding in or replacing the meat with vegetables like chopped, sautéed bell peppers and onions or chopped spinach. Be sure to use some type of muffin cup liner with these bad boys, or you will be scrubbing your muffin pan for days, as we learned the hard way. Silicone muffin liners are recommended because the paper liners can get soggy and stick to the muffins.

Yield: 12 mini casseroles

4–5 slices whole wheat bread, torn into ½" pieces (enough to fill muffin cups two-thirds full)

4 slices deli ham, chopped into small pieces

1 cup shredded Cheddar cheese

8 large eggs

1 cup whole milk

2 teaspoons ground mustard (optional)

½ teaspoon ground black pepper

1 teaspoon dried parsley flakes

GOES WELL WITH

✓ Apple Maple Sausage Patties (page 56)

✓ Fresh fruit or fruit salad

1. Preheat the oven to 400°F. Coat a 12-cup muffin pan with cooking spray. Place liners in the muffin cups.

2. Divide the bread pieces evenly among the muffin cups until each is about two-thirds full. Sprinkle the ham evenly over the bread. Sprinkle the cheese evenly over the ham.

3. In a measuring bowl with a spout, whisk together the eggs, milk, mustard (if using), and pepper. Pour the egg mixture evenly into each muffin cup.

4. Sprinkle the parsley on the top of each muffin. (*Freezing instructions begin here.*)

5. Bake for 15 to 18 minutes, or until golden brown on top and the middles are set.

Freezer Meal Instructions

TO FREEZE: Follow directions through Step 4. Do not bake. Place the muffin pan in the freezer to flash freeze the mini casseroles. Once the cups are thoroughly frozen, either wrap the entire pan tightly with plastic wrap and foil or remove the mini casseroles from muffin pan and place in an airtight freezer container.

TO PREPARE FROM FROZEN: Place frozen mini casseroles back into muffin pan, if removed, and let muffins thaw completely in fridge. Before baking, set on the counter for about 30 minutes to bring up to room temperature. At this point, go back to Step 5.

BLUEBERRY AVOCADO MUFFINS WITH LEMON STREUSEL TOPPING

I know what you're thinking. "Avocado? In a muffin? Ladies, you've gone too far." Before you move on, allow me to make a case for these muffins. They are delish! We had quite a few of our blog readers test them to make sure we weren't too wacky. They confirmed that these are a hit—even with their kids! The avocado is virtually tasteless and replaces the oil and butter that is usually found in muffins. To hide the hint of green that might throw a picky eater off, simply add the sweet and zesty crumble topping. —POLLY Yield: 15 muffins

MUFFINS

1 cup unbleached all-purpose flour

¾ cup whole wheat flour

¼ cup ground flaxseed

2 teaspoons baking powder

½ teaspoon baking soda

½ teaspoon salt

1 large, ripe Hass avocado, pitted

¾ cup sugar

1 large egg

1 teaspoon vanilla extract

1 cup plain Greek yogurt

1½ cups fresh blueberries

LEMON STREUSEL TOPPING (OPTIONAL)

¼ cup whole wheat flour

⅓ cup sugar

1 teaspoon grated lemon zest

3 tablespoons unsalted butter, cut into small pieces

1. To make the muffins: Preheat the oven to 375°F. Place silicone or paper liners in 15 cups in muffin pans or coat the cups with cooking spray.

2. In a medium bowl, mix together the flours, flaxseed, baking powder, baking soda, and salt.

3. Spoon the avocado flesh into the bowl of a stand mixer with a beater attachment. Beat on low until almost smooth. (If you don't have a stand mixer, simply mash up the avocado as much as possible with a fork.) With the mixer still running on low, add the sugar. Once the sugar is mixed in, beat in the egg. Add the vanilla and yogurt and mix well.

4. Slowly add the flour mixture to the wet ingredients and mix until just blended, being sure not to overmix. At this point, the batter will be a bit thick. Using a spoon, gently fold in the blueberries.

5. Fill the muffin cups about three-fourths full, leaving room for the streusel topping.

6. To make the streusel topping: In a medium bowl, combine the flour, sugar, and lemon zest. Using a pastry cutter or a fork, cut in the butter until it resembles coarse crumbles.

(CONTINUED)

✓ Spinach and Bacon
  Quiche (recipe
  available on
  Thriving Home)

✓ Oven Omelet
  (recipe available on
  Thriving Home)

✓ Cantaloupe

7. Sprinkle the streusel topping evenly over the batter.

8. Bake for 25 to 30 minutes, or until a toothpick inserted in the center of a muffin comes out clean. Let the muffins cool in the pan on a rack for 5 to 10 minutes before removing. (*Freezing instructions begin here.*)

9. Serve warm or at room temperature.

Freezer Meal Instructions

TO FREEZE: After the muffins have cooled, place them in an airtight freezer container or freezer bag.

TO PREPARE FROM FROZEN: Wrap a frozen muffin in a moist paper towel and microwave in 30- to 60-second increments until warmed all the way through.

Cooking Notes

▶ If you want to use frozen blueberries, just toss them in a bit of flour before stirring them into the mixture. This will prevent them from sinking to the bottom.

▶ The streusel topping is optional. Feel free to leave it off if you are trying to avoid added sugar.

PUMPKIN MUFFINS WITH CRUMBLE TOPPING

Over the years, I've become sort of a muffin snob. After testing dozens of muffin recipes, I can confidently say that this is one of my, as well as Thriving Home readers', all-time favorites. We just couldn't write a cookbook without including it. The muffins' soft, moist texture is perfectly complemented by the crunchy, sweet crumble topping. Plus, with all the autumn-inspired spices, these surprisingly nutritious muffins pack a delightful "pumpkin pie" punch. —POLLY Yield: 24 muffins

MUFFINS

- 1½ cups whole wheat flour
- 1 cup unbleached all-purpose flour
- ½ cup old-fashioned rolled oats
- 3½ teaspoons ground cinnamon
- ½ teaspoon ground nutmeg
- ¼ teaspoon ground cloves
- ½ teaspoon ground ginger
- 2 teaspoons baking soda
- 1 teaspoon baking powder
- ½ teaspoon salt
- 1 can (15 ounces) pumpkin puree
- 1 cup granulated sugar
- ⅔ cup melted coconut oil
- ½ cup applesauce
- 3 large eggs
- 1 teaspoon vanilla extract

CRUMBLE TOPPING (OPTIONAL, BUT RECOMMENDED)

- ¼ cup brown sugar
- 2 tablespoons butter, softened
- ¼ cup old-fashioned rolled oats
- 2 tablespoons whole wheat flour

1. **To make the muffins:** Preheat the oven to 350°F. Place paper or silicone liners in two 12-cup muffin pans or coat with cooking spray.

2. In a medium mixing bowl, combine the flours, oats, cinnamon, nutmeg, cloves, ginger, baking soda, baking powder, and salt.

3. In a large mixing bowl, whisk together the pumpkin, granulated sugar, coconut oil, applesauce, eggs, and vanilla.

4. Add the flour mixture to the pumpkin mixture and stir just until combined.

5. Pour the batter into the muffin cups, filling each about two-thirds full.

6. **To make the crumble topping:** In a small bowl, mix the brown sugar and butter together until creamy and smooth. Using a fork, stir in the oats and flour until the mixture is crumbly.

7. Sprinkle each muffin evenly with the crumble topping.

8. Bake for about 18 minutes, or until a toothpick inserted in the center of a muffin comes out clean.

(CONTINUED)

GOES WELL WITH

✓ Apple Maple
Sausage Bites
(page 56)

✓ Scrambled eggs

✓ Fresh fruit salad

✓ Coffee!

Freezer Meal Instructions

TO FREEZE: Bake and completely cool the muffins. Then place them in an airtight freezer container or bag and freeze.

TO PREPARE FROM FROZEN: Either let muffins thaw at room temperature or wrap them in a moist paper towel and microwave in 30-second intervals until warmed all the way through.

BUSY MORNING BREAKFAST COOKIES

Getting a healthy breakfast on the table in the midst of hungry little people who are still fighting off the sleep-grumps proves to be quite a challenge. The truth is, with kids or not, mornings go by quickly. These breakfast cookies make perfect sense to have in the freezer for a quick and filling meal. Packed into all of these nutritious ingredients are pops of flavor that give some of the sweetness you expect in a cookie. Double and freeze a batch so you have some on hand for your next busy morning. *Yield: 24 cookies*

½ cup butter, softened

½ cup firmly packed dark brown sugar

1 teaspoon vanilla extract

1 can (20 ounces) crushed pineapple, drained

1 cup whole wheat flour

1 cup unbleached all-purpose flour

1 teaspoon baking soda

1 teaspoon ground cinnamon

¼ teaspoon salt

1¾ cups rolled oats

1 cup golden raisins

1 cup chopped pecans or walnuts

1. Preheat the oven to 350°F. Coat a foil-lined baking sheet with cooking spray or cover with parchment paper.

2. In a large mixing bowl, combine the butter, brown sugar, vanilla, and pineapple.

3. In a medium mixing bowl, combine the flours, baking soda, cinnamon, salt, oats, raisins, and nuts.

4. Add the dry ingredients to the pineapple mixture and stir until well combined.

5. Drop rounded spoonfuls of batter onto the baking sheet. Using a fork, press cookie dough down a bit to resemble more of a cookie shape. *(Freezing instructions for Method 1 begin here.)*

6. Bake for 13 minutes, or until the middles of the cookies are firm to the touch. Let cool before removing from the baking sheet. *(Freezing instructions for Method 2 begin here.)*

Freezer Meal Instructions

TO FREEZE

METHOD 1: Make the cookie dough and scoop onto the baking sheet. Place the baking sheet into the freezer to flash freeze the dough, about 1 hour. Once the dough is frozen, transfer to a plastic freezer bag and store in the freezer.

METHOD 2: Fully bake and cool cookies. Then place in an airtight freezer bag or container and freeze.

(CONTINUED)

✓ Oven Omelet
   (recipe available on
   Thriving Home)

✓ Fresh pineapple
   slices

✓ Yogurt

TO PREPARE FROM FROZEN

METHOD 1: Take desired amount of cookie dough balls out of the freezer and let them thaw in the fridge overnight or at room temperature for 10 to 15 minutes. Bake as directed.

METHOD 2: Let cookies thaw on the countertop, or microwave a cookie in 10-second intervals until warmed up.

Cooking Notes

▶ Substitute any small dried fruit for the golden raisins.

▶ To add some sweetness, toss in $1/2$ cup dark chocolate chips.

▶ These also make a great afterschool snack.

HASH BROWN BREAKFAST BAKE

With shredded potatoes, eggs, bacon, and cheese, this recipe leaves everyone feeling satisfied at breakfast. Or serve this crowd-pleaser casserole with a side salad and some fresh fruit for an easy-peasy dinner. If you prefer, you can replace bacon with chopped ham or substitute Cheddar with your favorite shredded cheese. If you want to downsize the dish, simply split the casserole into two 8″ x 8″ dishes and freeze one for later. *Yield: 12 servings*

2 teaspoons olive or avocado oil

1 small yellow onion, finely chopped

4 cloves garlic, minced

1 pound frozen shredded hash browns

1 pound bacon, cooked and chopped

3 cups shredded Cheddar cheese

2 tablespoons minced fresh chives

⅓ cup packed fresh parsley, finely chopped

12 large eggs

2 cups milk

1 teaspoon salt

½ teaspoon ground black pepper

GOES WELL WITH

✓ Zucchini Flaxseed Muffins (recipe available on Thriving Home)

✓ Blueberry Avocado Muffins (page 42)

✓ Fresh Fruit

1. Preheat the oven to 350°F. Coat a 13″ x 9″ or two 8″ x 8″ baking dishes with cooking spray.

2. In a medium skillet, heat the oil over medium-high heat. Cook the onion, stirring frequently, until soft, about 5 minutes. Stir in the garlic during the last 30 seconds of cooking time.

3. In a large mixing bowl, combine the onion mixture, frozen hash browns, cooked bacon, cheese, chives, and parsley.

4. In a medium mixing bowl, whisk together the eggs, milk, salt, and pepper. Pour over the hash brown mixture. Stir until well combined. Pour into the baking dish (or dishes). *(Freezing instructions begin here.)*

5. Bake for 55 to 65 minutes, or until the center is set and the top is golden brown. Let cool for a few minutes before serving.

Freezer Meal Instructions

TO FREEZE: Put the casserole together but do not bake. Wrap the unbaked casserole tightly and freeze.

TO PREPARE FROM FROZEN: Let the casserole thaw in the refrigerator completely. This may take up to 24 hours or more. Bake according to directions.

Cooking Notes

▶ If you don't have peaches on hand, apples will work great!

▶ Toss in some dried cranberries for extra sweetness and flavor.

▶ Leftovers can be stored in the fridge for 5 to 7 days. When reheating, stir in extra milk before microwaving since the oatmeal will lose some moisture.

PEACHES AND CREAM BAKED OATMEAL

Over the years, baked oatmeal has become a much-loved breakfast in my home. It has entirely replaced the sugar-laden oatmeal packets I used to get at the store. Since peaches and cream was my favorite oatmeal flavor as a kid, it felt only natural to create a whole foods version. This recipe is very filling and a win with all ages. The peaches provide juicy sweetness, while the pecans add a nice crunch. Don't forget to top it off with some warm milk when serving to make it nice and creamy. —POLLY Yield: 6 servings

---

3 cups old-fashioned rolled oats

½ cup firmly packed dark brown sugar

¼ cup ground flaxseed

1 teaspoon salt

1 teaspoon baking powder

1 teaspoon ground cinnamon

½ cup pecans, chopped

½ cup melted coconut oil or melted butter

¼ cup pure maple syrup

2 large eggs

1 cup milk, plus more for serving

2 cups chopped fresh or frozen peaches (about 2 large peaches)

GOES WELL WITH

✓ Oven Omelet (recipe available on Thriving Home)

---

1. Preheat the oven to 350°F. Grease a 13″ x 9″ or two 8″ x 8″ baking dishes with cooking spray.

2. In a large bowl, combine the oats, brown sugar, flaxseed, salt, baking powder, cinnamon, and pecans.

3. Drizzle the coconut oil or butter over the dry ingredients and stir until well combined. (This prevents the oil from coagulating in the wet ingredients.)

4. In a separate bowl, whisk together the maple syrup, eggs, and milk.

5. Add the wet ingredients to the oats mixture and stir together until well combined. Stir in the peaches.

6. Spread the mixture out in the baking dish (or dishes). *(Freezing instructions begin here.)* Bake for 20 to 25 minutes, or until the middle is mostly set.

7. Serve warm with a splash of milk poured over the top.

Freezer Meal Instructions

TO FREEZE: Follow the recipe instructions through Step 6, but do not bake. Cover the top of the baking dish with either a lid or plastic wrap and foil. Freeze.

TO PREPARE FROM FROZEN: Let the dish thaw in the refrigerator. Bake as instructed above.

BANANA CHOCOLATE CHIP BREAKFAST CAKE

I've been making a breakfast cake like this for years for my family. Think moist, sweet banana bread in cake form. We like it warmed slightly with a little butter, cream cheese, or even peanut butter on top. The best part: It is filled with banana and sneaky sweet potato, lower in sugar than most sweet breads, and partially made with whole wheat flour. One key to making this cake light is using the white whole wheat variety, if you can find it. You could even use all white whole wheat flour if you want to make this 100 percent whole grain. For breakfast, a snack, or dessert, this cake makes the cut. —RACHEL *Yield: 9 servings*

---

2 large overripe bananas, mashed

1 medium sweet potato, cooked and mashed (about ¾–1 cup)

2 large eggs

1 teaspoon vanilla extract

⅓ cup melted coconut oil

½ cup plain Greek yogurt

1 cup whole wheat flour (recommended: King Arthur White Whole Wheat)

1 cup unbleached all-purpose flour

½ cup sugar

1 teaspoon baking powder

1 teaspoon baking soda

½ teaspoon salt

½ cup mini chocolate chips

1. Coat an 8" x 8" ceramic, dark metal, or glass baking dish with cooking spray. Preheat the oven to 350°F for a ceramic or dark metal dish or 325°F for a glass dish.

2. In a blender, combine the bananas, sweet potato, eggs, vanilla, coconut oil, and yogurt. Blend until smooth.

3. In a large bowl, whisk together the flours, sugar, baking powder, baking soda, and salt until thoroughly mixed.

4. Using a spatula to clean out the blender, add the wet ingredients to the dry ingredients. Stir gently with a spoon just until combined (do not overmix). Batter will be thick.

5. Gently stir in the chocolate chips until just combined.

6. Pour the batter into the baking dish and spread evenly with a spatula.

7. Bake for 35 to 40 minutes for a ceramic or dark metal dish or 45 to 50 minutes for a glass dish, or until a toothpick comes out clean in the center. Do not overbake. *(Freezing instructions begin here.)*

8. Serve warm slices of cake with a little butter or cream cheese on top.

GOES WELL WITH

✓ Apple Maple
Sausage Bites
(page 56)

✓ No Fail Bacon
(recipe available on
Thriving Home)

✓ Fresh Fruit or Fruit
Salad

Freezer Meal Instructions

TO FREEZE: Bake just until done. Cool completely. Either cover the baking dish tightly in a few layers of foil or plastic wrap or carefully lift the cake out of the baking dish and wrap in several layers of foil or plastic wrap, pressing out all the air. Freeze.

TO PREPARE FROM FROZEN: Thaw on the counter. Warm a slice in the microwave for 15 to 30 seconds and top with a pat of butter, if desired.

Cooking Notes

▶ If you don't have a blender, a potato masher can work. Simply mash up the bananas and sweet potato in a bowl before stirring in the other wet ingredients.

CINNAMON OATMEAL PANCAKE MIX

Since the day my sister introduced me to oatmeal pancakes, I have never gone back to my quick-mix boxed recipes. These will change your life, I tell you. They are hearty, flavorful, and full of whole grains that won't leave you hungry hours later. I usually make a huge batch of dry mix and just keep it tucked in the back of my freezer for mornings when my kids are clamoring for pancakes. For a sweeter treat, sprinkle mini chocolate chips over the pancake batter as it's cooking. —POLLY Yield: 2½ cups dry mix (enough for about 10 pancakes)

1 cup old-fashioned rolled oats

1¼ cups whole wheat flour

1 tablespoon brown sugar

1 tablespoon ground cinnamon

1½ teaspoons baking powder

¾ teaspoon salt

¾ teaspoon baking soda

¼ cup melted coconut oil

1 large egg

1 cup whole milk

GOES WELL WITH

✓ No Fail Bacon (recipe available on Thriving Home)

✓ Apple Maple Sausage Bites (page 56)

✓ Fresh fruit

1. *To assemble mix:* In a food processor, process the oats until they resemble a coarse sand (about 30 seconds).

2. In a large mixing bowl, mix together the processed oats, flour, brown sugar, cinnamon, baking powder, salt, and baking soda.

3. While stirring, drizzle in the coconut oil. Stir until thoroughly mixed in. *(Freezing instructions begin here for Method 1.)*

4. *To make the pancakes:* In a large bowl, combine the pancake mix, egg, and milk.

5. Heat a large nonstick skillet over medium heat and coat with cooking spray. Pour about ⅓ cup of batter per pancake into the skillet, making sure not to overcrowd the pan. Cook for about 4 minutes, turning once, or until each side is slightly browned. *(Freezing instructions begin here for Method 2.)*

6. Serve with butter and pure maple syrup on top.

Freezer Meal Instructions

TO FREEZE

METHOD 1: After assembling the dry mix, freeze it in an airtight container (without the egg and milk).

METHOD 2: Cook the pancakes and cool completely on a cooling rack. Place pancakes in single layers in gallon-size freezer bags with parchment paper between layers. Seal tightly and freeze.

TO PREPARE FROM FROZEN

METHOD 1: Use frozen pancake mix as directed. No need to thaw.

METHOD 2: Place frozen pancakes in the toaster for one cycle. Then microwave in 10-second increments until heated through.

APPLE MAPLE SAUSAGE BITES

Most store-bought breakfast sausage patties are loaded with sodium, MSG, and other questionable ingredients. That's why we love this easy, all-natural homemade version. These protein-rich, slightly sweet sausage bites leave you satiated all morning long and are a great side to almost every breakfast item in our book, but especially the Cinnamon Oatmeal Pancakes (page 54). Thanks to our friend Kelly at Nourishing Home for the recipe inspiration!

Yield: about 25 patties

½ cup grated apple

1 teaspoon ground sage

½ teaspoon celery salt

½ teaspoon onion powder

¼ teaspoon ground cayenne pepper

¼ teaspoon dried thyme

½ tablespoon brown sugar

½ teaspoon salt

½ teaspoon ground black pepper

1¼ pounds ground pork or ground turkey

2 cloves garlic, minced

1½ tablespoons pure maple syrup

2 tablespoons butter

GOES WELL WITH

✓ Cinnamon Oatmeal Pancakes (page 54)

✓ Chocolate Zu-Nana Waffles (page 58)

✓ Blueberry Avocado Muffins (page 42)

1. In a small bowl, mix together the apple, sage, celery salt, onion powder, cayenne pepper, thyme, brown sugar, salt, and black pepper.

2. Place the pork or turkey in a large bowl and sprinkle the seasoning mixture over the top. Add the garlic and maple syrup and stir (or use your hands to mix) until the seasonings are thoroughly distributed.

3. Using your hands, form the meat mixture into 1½"-wide patties that are about ½" thick. *(Freezing instructions begin here.)*

4. In a large skillet, melt 1 tablespoon of the butter over medium heat. Add half of the patties, making sure they don't touch. Cook for 4 to 6 minutes, turning once, or until no longer pink. Repeat with the remaining butter and patties.

Freezer Meal Instructions

TO FREEZE: Place uncooked sausage patties in a gallon-size freezer bag or a freezer container in single layers. Separate layers with parchment paper. Squeeze out all the air, seal tightly, and freeze for up to 4 months.

TO PREPARE FROM FROZEN: Thaw frozen patties in the refrigerator overnight. Follow cooking instructions in Step 4.

Cooking Notes

▶ When forming patties, wet your hands with water to prevent sticking.

▶ If your apples are extra juicy, use a paper towel to absorb some of the extra moisture before mixing them in with the seasoning ingredients.

APPLE RAISIN BAKED FRENCH TOAST

Here's a breakfast that is ready to pop in the oven as soon as you wake up. The aroma of cooked apples, sweet cinnamon, and warm bread is a welcoming scent as family members begin to filter into the kitchen for the morning. Baked French toast is easy to assemble the night before, not to mention it's a great way to use up heels of bread that have been saved in the freezer. Turn that stale bread into this comforting, delicious breakfast in just a few simple steps! *Yield: 8 servings*

10 slices whole grain bread (or enough to fill a 13" x 9" baking dish), torn into small pieces

2 cups chopped apples (about 2 apples; no need to peel)

½ cup raisins

2 cups milk

8 large eggs

¼ cup butter, melted

¼ cup pure maple syrup

2 teaspoons vanilla extract

2 tablespoons firmly packed brown sugar

2 teaspoons ground cinnamon

¼ teaspoon salt

½ cup chopped pecans

GOES WELL WITH

✓ No Fail Bacon (recipe available on Thriving Home)

✓ Apple Maple Sausage Bites (page 56)

1. Coat a 13" x 9" glass baking dish with cooking spray. In the dish, evenly spread out the torn bread pieces. Sprinkle the apples and raisins evenly over the top of the bread.

2. In a large bowl, whisk together the milk, eggs, butter, maple syrup, vanilla, brown sugar, cinnamon, and salt until well combined.

3. Pour the egg mixture over the top of the bread. Sprinkle the pecans on top. *(Freezing instructions begin here.)*

4. Refrigerate for 30 minutes or up to 24 hours.

5. Preheat the oven to 375°F. Bake for about 35 minutes, or until the egg mixture is set and the top is golden.

6. Serve warm. Add more butter and maple syrup, if desired.

Freezer Meal Instructions

TO FREEZE: Complete recipe through Step 3. Do not bake before freezing. Wrap baking dish tightly in a few layers of plastic wrap and one of foil and freeze.

TO PREPARE FROM FROZEN: Thaw in the fridge for about 24 hours and bake according to recipe directions. Or defrost in the microwave and then bake. To bake from frozen, cover dish with foil and plan to bake longer, until the middle is cooked through.

Cooking Notes

▶ Recipe could make two 8" x 8" pans instead of one 13" x 9".

▶ Sprinkle ¼ cup ground flaxseed over the top for more of a crust.

▶ Add ½ cup pumpkin puree to the egg mixture before pouring it over the bread.

CHOCOLATE ZU-NANA WAFFLES

My kids let out a cheer when they see these waffles on the menu. (Do they really need to know they're loaded with zucchini, bananas, whole wheat, and flaxseed?) In the summer months when zucchini takes over my garden, I shred and freeze it in small portions. And when my bananas begin to go bad, I peel and freeze those, too. It never hurts to be prepared with ingredients to make this "breakfast for dinner" favorite. —RACHEL

Yield: 18 (4" x 4") waffles

---

2 overripe bananas, smashed

¼ cup melted coconut oil or melted butter

2 large eggs

1½ cups milk

1 teaspoon vanilla extract

1 cup shredded zucchini

1 cup whole wheat flour

½ cup unbleached all-purpose flour

2 tablespoons ground flaxseed

1 tablespoon baking powder

½ teaspoon baking soda

¼ teaspoon salt

½ cup unsweetened cocoa powder, sifted

½ cup mini chocolate chips

1. Preheat a waffle iron.

2. In a medium mixing bowl or a blender, combine the bananas, coconut oil or butter, eggs, milk, vanilla, and zucchini. Mix or blend well.

3. In a large mixing bowl, whisk together the flours, flaxseed, baking powder, baking soda, salt, and cocoa.

4. Pour the wet ingredients into the dry ingredients and stir just until combined. Do not overmix. Gently stir in the chocolate chips. Let the batter sit for a few minutes.

5. Coat the hot waffle iron with cooking spray. Add ¼ cup batter per waffle. Cook for about 3 minutes, or according to the waffle iron manufacturer's directions. *(Freezing instructions begin here.)* If desired, serve with butter or peanut butter and a little maple syrup on top.

Freezer Meal Instructions

TO FREEZE: Make and cool waffles completely on a cooling rack. Place waffles in single layers in gallon-size freezer bags with parchment paper between layers. Seal tightly and freeze.

TO PREPARE FROM FROZEN: Toast frozen waffles. If still slightly cold inside, microwave in 10-second increments until warmed through.

(CONTINUED)

Cooking Notes

▶ Use the grating blade on a food processor to quickly shred zucchini.

▶ If using frozen and thawed zucchini, squeeze out the excess moisture.

GOES WELL WITH

✓ Apple Maple Sausage Bites (page 56)

✓ No Fail Bacon (recipe available on Thriving Home)

✓ Fresh fruit or fruit salad

MIXED BERRY OAT SCONES

Enjoying a yummy baked treat while sipping coffee in the morning is good for my soul. Since I'm a sucker for a morning pastry, having a go-to scone recipe is a must. The berries—whichever ones you like the best or whatever is in season—add moisture and pops of fruity goodness to these scrumptious scones. Do keep in mind that flour is your friend when pressing these out. Make sure your surface and hands are well floured to avoid getting yourself in a sticky situation! We highly recommend using the white whole wheat flour variety to maintain a light texture. —**POLLY** Yield: 16 scones

SCONES

1 cup white whole wheat flour

1 cup unbleached all-purpose flour

¾ cup old-fashioned rolled oats

1 tablespoon baking powder

⅓ cup granulated sugar

½ teaspoon salt

½ cup cold butter, cut into small pieces

1 cup heavy cream

1 egg

1½ cups frozen blueberries, raspberries, and/or strawberries

GLAZE (RECOMMENDED BUT OPTIONAL)

1 cup powdered sugar

2 tablespoons milk or heavy cream

½ teaspoon vanilla extract

Pinch of salt

1. *To make the scones:* Preheat the oven to 400°F. Line 2 baking sheets with parchment paper and set aside.

2. In a large bowl, whisk together the flours, oats, baking powder, granulated sugar, and salt. Using a pastry cutter (or just your hands if you don't have one), mix in the butter until the mixture resembles coarse crumbles.

3. In a small mixing bowl, whisk together the cream and egg until well blended.

4. Pour the wet mixture into the dry ingredients and stir until the dough starts to come together. (Be careful not to overmix. There should be some floury patches.) Gently stir in the frozen berries.

5. On a floured surface, turn the dough out and press it into a rectangle about ¾″ thick. Using a pizza cutter or knife, cut in half from shortest side to shortest side. Make 3 even cuts across the other direction. Now cut each square into triangles.

6. Transfer the scones to the baking sheets, leaving room between each. *(Freezing instructions for Method 1 begin here.)* Bake for 15 minutes, or until the tops start to brown. Transfer scones to a cooling rack.

7. *To make the glaze:* In a small bowl, mix together the powdered sugar, milk or cream, vanilla, and salt. Drizzle over the tops of the scones. *(Freezing instructions for Method 2 begin here.)*

(CONTINUED)

Freezer Meal Instructions

TO FREEZE

METHOD 1: Pop the baking sheets in the freezer and flash freeze for 2 to 3 hours, or until the scones are completely frozen. Place scones in an airtight freezer container or plastic freezer bag. Assemble glaze as directed in Step 7 and place it in a separate freezer bag. Freeze both scones and glaze together.

METHOD 2: Bake scones as directed. Let them cool and then place in an airtight container or gallon-size freezer bag and freeze. Assemble glaze as directed in Step 7 and place it in a separate freezer bag. Freeze scones and glaze together.

TO PREPARE FROM FROZEN

METHOD 1: Place frozen unbaked scones on a parchment-lined baking sheet and let thaw on the counter for 10 to 15 minutes. Bake as directed, adding a few additional minutes if needed. While scones are baking, let glaze thaw at room temperature. Once the scones have cooled, drizzle the glaze over the top.

METHOD 2: Let scones and glaze thaw at room temperature for 15 to 20 minutes. Microwave scone for about 30 seconds or until warm. Top with glaze.

SOUTHWEST BREAKFAST BURRITOS

Having a stash of breakfast burritos in the freezer sets us up for a smooth morning. Not only will these keep a belly full until lunch time, but they heat up quickly. We've provided a basic recipe with potatoes, eggs, cheese, and bacon, but feel free to tinker around with the recipe to make it a win for your own family. You can easily swap in cooked breakfast sausage for the bacon and add sautéed peppers and onions. Yield: 8 burritos

12 large eggs

1 teaspoon salt

½ teaspoon ground black pepper

½ cup milk

1 can (4 ounces) chopped green chile peppers, drained

1½ tablespoons butter

2 cups shredded Cheddar cheese

½ cup all-natural salsa (optional)

1 pound frozen shredded or diced potatoes, cooked according to package instructions

1 pound cooked bacon, chopped

8 wheat tortillas (10–12″ diameter)

GOES WELL WITH

✓ Homemade Guacamole (recipe available on Thriving Home)

1. Preheat the oven to 350°F. In a large bowl, whisk together the eggs, salt, black pepper, milk, and chile peppers until blended.

2. In a large nonstick skillet, melt the butter over medium heat, making sure it does not brown. Pour in the egg mixture and scramble the eggs until set but still moist. Remove from the heat and set aside.

3. Prepare an assembly line with all ingredients. Assemble each burrito by placing approximately ½ cup eggs, ¼ cup cheese, 1 tablespoon salsa (if using), ⅓ cup potatoes, and 2 tablespoons bacon in the middle of a tortilla, leaving 1″ of space at the top and bottom and 1½″ on the left and right. Use a spoon or your hands to toss the ingredients before wrapping the tortilla.

4. Fold the bottom of the tortilla up onto the filling. Holding the bottom flap in place, fold the top of the tortilla over the ingredients. Hold flaps down and fold left-hand side over ingredients, tucking it under. Roll burrito until right-hand side is wrapped around, and then let the burrito rest on the seam to seal the burrito. Wrap burritos tightly in foil. (*Freezing instructions begin here.*)

5. Bake for 10 minutes.

Freezer Meal Instructions

TO FREEZE: Place foil-wrapped burritos in a freezer bag and freeze.

TO PREPARE FROM FROZEN: Unwrap the foil from the frozen burrito, wrap in a moist paper towel, and microwave using the defrost setting for 2 to 3 minutes, or until warmed through. Or bake the foil-wrapped frozen burrito in a 350°F oven for about 20 minutes, or until warmed through.

Crispy Chicken with
Lemony Butter Sauce, *page 76*

CHAPTER 5

chicken

CILANTRO LIME CHICKEN

This marinade transforms the humble chicken breast with bold, bright flavors like fresh lime juice, citruslike cilantro, sweet honey, and red-pepper flakes. Cilantro Lime Chicken is one of those staple recipes that can be used in a variety of ways. Whether served in a wrap with your favorite Mexican toppings, thinly sliced and tossed over a salad, or chopped up and used on baked nachos, this recipe never fails to please a crowd, no matter the age.

Yield: 3–4 servings

¼ cup packed cilantro, chopped

3 tablespoons soy sauce

2 tablespoons honey

1 tablespoon olive oil or avocado oil

Juice of 1 lime (about 2 tablespoons)

2 cloves garlic, minced

1 tablespoon cumin

1 teaspoon salt

½ teaspoon red-pepper flakes

1½ pounds boneless, skinless chicken breasts

GOES WELL WITH

✓ Avocado Lime Salsa (recipe available on Thriving Home)

✓ Guacamole (recipe available on Thriving Home)

✓ Baked Nachos (recipe available on Thriving Home)

1. In a gallon-size resealable freezer bag, combine the cilantro, soy sauce, honey, olive or avocado oil, lime juice, garlic, cumin, salt, and red-pepper flakes. Seal and shake to combine thoroughly. Add the chicken and coat with the marinade. Squeeze out the air and seal tightly. *(Freezing instructions begin here.)*

2. Let the chicken marinate in the refrigerator for at least 2 hours and up to 24 hours.

3. Choose a cooking method:

METHOD 1: Preheat a grill or grill pan to medium-high heat. Grill for 12 to 14 minutes, turning once, or until a thermometer inserted in the thickest portion registers 165°F and the juices run clear.

METHOD 2: Preheat the oven to 375°F. Coat a rimmed baking sheet with cooking spray or line it with foil. Place the chicken breasts on top, making sure they don't touch. Roast for about 25 minutes, turning once, or until a thermometer inserted in the thickest portion registers 165°F and the juices run clear.

4. To serve: Eat the chicken as is or use it to make wraps, tacos, nachos, salads, sandwiches, or in any other way you want to prepare it.

Freezer Meal Instructions

TO FREEZE: Assemble marinade as directed. Add chicken to the marinade and freeze in a gallon-size freezer bag or container.

TO PREPARE FROM FROZEN: Let chicken and marinade thaw in refrigerator for 24 hours (or until completely thawed). Cook as directed.

CHICKEN PARMESAN CASSEROLE

We simply couldn't write a cookbook without including this freezer meal, which came in as the most popular recipe on Thriving Home. Lean chicken, your favorite marinara sauce, two kinds of cheese, and a quick bread crumb and herb topping make for a well-rounded, simple casserole that can stand alone or go on top of whole grain pasta or rice. One once-skeptical reader commented, "My family considers this a favorite recipe. I make large quantities of marinara sauce and store it in the freezer, which comes in handy when making Chicken Parm. I'm not a 'casserole' person, so I wasn't sold on the idea of Chicken Parm Casserole, but this casserole recipe somehow works. Thanks for sharing. It's delicious!" *Yield: 6 servings*

---

4 cups (about 1½ pounds) shredded or cubed cooked chicken

3 cups Slow Cooker Marinara Sauce (page 212)

½ cup grated Parmesan cheese

1½ cups shredded mozzarella cheese

1 cup whole wheat panko bread crumbs

1–2 tablespoons olive oil

¼ cup packed fresh parsley, minced

1 teaspoon salt

½ teaspoon ground black pepper

Cooked whole wheat pasta (optional)

GOES WELL WITH

✓ Garlic Herb Butter for Bread (recipe available on Thriving Home)

✓ Salad

1. Preheat the oven to 350°F. Coat an 8″ x 8″ casserole dish with cooking spray.

2. Place the chicken in the bottom of the pan in an even layer. Next spread the marinara sauce over the chicken. Top the marinara with the Parmesan and then the mozzarella.

3. In a small bowl, mix the bread crumbs, olive oil, parsley, salt, and pepper together. Sprinkle over the top of the casserole. *(Freezer instructions begin here.)*

4. Bake for 20 to 25 minutes, or until golden on top and bubbling on the sides. Serve over whole wheat pasta, if desired.

Freezer Meal Instructions

TO FREEZE: Assemble casserole as directed, but do not bake. Wrap dish in plastic wrap and foil or cover tightly with an airtight lid. Freeze.

TO PREPARE FROM FROZEN: Let the casserole thaw in the refrigerator. Bake as directed.

Cooking Notes

▶ This is a great way to use up leftover chicken!

▶ For some extra nutrition, toss in some chopped fresh spinach after adding the marinara.

PARMESAN AND HERB CHICKEN TENDERS

Who doesn't love a good chicken tender? From fast-food chains to school cafeterias, chicken tenders are available almost anywhere. While we may love them, most are deep-fried in trans fats, loaded with processed ingredients, and made from suspect meat (what part of the chicken is it *really* from?). The good news is that these oven-baked tenders are packed with whole, fresh ingredients and maintain a nice crisp texture. Keep a bag of them on hand in the freezer for a quick, nutritious lunch or dinner anytime.

Yield: 4 servings (about 3 tenders per person)

1½ pounds chicken tenders or 1½ pounds boneless, skinless chicken breasts, cut into 1" strips

Salt and ground black pepper

1 cup whole wheat flour

2 large eggs

¼ cup water

2 cups whole wheat bread crumbs

1 cup grated Parmesan cheese

Leaves from 6 sprigs fresh thyme, finely chopped (about 1 tablespoon)

Leaves from 6 sprigs fresh rosemary, finely chopped (about 1–2 tablespoons)

2 handfuls flat-leaf parsley leaves, finely chopped

1 teaspoon garlic powder

½ teaspoon red-pepper flakes (optional)

1. Preheat the oven to 425°F. Place a foil-lined baking sheet in the oven to preheat. (A hot baking sheet helps the tenders stay nice and crisp!)

2. Season the chicken on both sides with salt and black pepper.

3. Place the flour in a shallow dish. In another shallow dish, beat the eggs with the water. In a third dish, combine the bread crumbs, cheese, herbs, garlic powder, and red-pepper flakes.

4. Coat the chicken with the flour. Dip it in the egg mixture, and then dredge it in the bread crumb mixture. Really press in the bread crumbs to make them stick! (*Freezing instructions begin here.*)

5. Remove the hot baking sheet from the oven and coat it with cooking spray. Place the chicken tenders on it and coat the tops with cooking spray. Bake for about 15 minutes, turning once, or until the chicken is no longer pink and the juices run clear. Serve immediately.

GOES WELL WITH

✓ Super Stuffed
  Baked Potatoes
  (page 121)

✓ Cheesy Mashed
  Sweet Potatoes
  (recipe available on
  Thriving Home)

✓ Corn on the cob

✓ Garden salad

Freezer Meal Instructions

TO FREEZE: Freeze breaded, uncooked chicken tenders in single layers in an airtight freezer container or a gallon-size freezer bag. Use parchment paper to separate layers, if necessary.

TO PREPARE FROM FROZEN: Place frozen chicken on a preheated, foil-lined baking sheet coated with cooking spray. Bake at 425°F for 20 to 25 minutes, turning once, or until the chicken is no longer pink and the juices run clear.

Cooking Notes

▶ If your kids are skeptical of green in their meals, throw the herbs in the food processor with the bread crumbs to blend them in better.

▶ Use these tenders on top of a salad for some added protein or in a wrap for a quick and yummy lunch.

CHICKEN AND BROCCOLI FOIL PACKS

If an all-in-one meal of brown rice, chicken, broccoli, cheese, and bacon is wrong, then we don't want to be right. Whether you are grilling out or just want a fun way to serve individually portioned meals, these foil packs prove to be a big win for kids, college students, parents, you name it. The mouth-watering ingredients melt into each other and share flavors as they cook. Perhaps the best part is that cleanup is a cinch! Yield: 6 servings

1–1½ pounds boneless, skinless chicken breasts, cut into bite-size pieces

1 teaspoon salt

½ teaspoon ground black pepper

1 teaspoon garlic powder

1 teaspoon onion powder

3 cups cooked brown rice

6 tablespoons butter

4 cups broccoli florets

2 cups shredded Cheddar cheese

1 pound bacon, cooked and chopped

1. Preheat the oven to 400°F or preheat a grill to medium-high heat. Season the chicken pieces with the salt, pepper, garlic powder, and onion powder. Set aside.

2. On a piece of heavy-duty foil, scoop ¹/₂ cup of the cooked rice. Top rice with 1 tablespoon of the butter. Add about ¹/₂ cup of the chicken. Top with ²/₃ cup of the broccoli, ¹/₃ cup of the cheese, and about 3 tablespoons of the bacon.

3. Bring up the sides of the foil and close up at the top. Make sure to leave room for heat circulation inside and a little opening at the top for steam to release. *(Freezing instructions begin here.)*

4. If baking, place the foil packs in a single layer on a baking sheet or in a baking dish. If grilling, place directly on the grill. Bake or grill for 20 to 25 minutes, or until a thermometer inserted in the chicken registers 165°F and the juices run clear.

5. Remove the foil packs from the heat and let stand for 5 to 7 minutes. Carefully open each pack to release the steam.

Freezer Meal Instructions

TO FREEZE: Follow the directions through Step 3, but do not cook. Instead, close up the foil packs tightly and place them in a large freezer bag or a container and freeze.

TO PREPARE FROM FROZEN: Let pack(s) thaw in the refrigerator for 24 hours. Open each foil pack a little at the top (to allow the steam to release when it cooks). Cook as directed, adding another 5 to 10 minutes to the cooking time.

Cooking Note

▶ Add a little Parmesan to add a bit more depth to the flavor.

CRISPY CHICKEN WITH LEMONY BUTTER SAUCE

This French-inspired dish is a nod to the classic chicken piccata but updated with a crispy crust and a simple yet elegant sauce that anyone can make. One of the keys to creating depth of flavor is seasoning the ingredients each step of the way.

Don't skimp on buying fresh lemons and good-quality white wine. The lemon juice and wine reduce in the sauce and marry with the butter to create something heavenly. Finish with a sprinkling of fresh chopped parsley over the top for a beautiful dish that's worthy of serving your best guests or for a simple sit-down family meal. *Yield: 4 servings*

1¼–1½ pounds boneless, skinless chicken breasts

Salt and ground black pepper

½ cup whole wheat flour

1 large egg

2 tablespoons water

1¼ cups whole wheat panko bread crumbs

½ teaspoon garlic powder

2 teaspoons dried parsley, crushed in hand

2 tablespoons olive oil or avocado oil, divided

6 tablespoons unsalted butter, at room temperature, divided

Juice of 2 medium lemons (about 4 tablespoons; reserve lemon halves)

1 cup good-quality dry white wine

2 tablespoons chopped fresh parsley, plus more for garnish

Sliced lemon, for garnish

1. Preheat the oven to 400°F. Line a sheet pan with parchment paper or foil.

2. Cut the chicken breasts in half horizontally. To do this, place your palm firmly on top of the chicken breast and slice in half with a sawing motion using a very sharp knife. Sprinkle both sides lightly with salt and pepper.

3. In a shallow dish, combine the flour, ½ teaspoon salt, and ¼ teaspoon pepper. In a second dish, beat the egg and water together. In a third dish, combine the bread crumbs, garlic powder, and dried parsley. Dip the chicken first in the flour, then in the egg, and lastly in the bread crumb mixture, pressing it on the chicken so it sticks. (*Freezing instructions begin here.*)

4. In a large skillet, heat 1 tablespoon of the oil over medium heat. Cook half the chicken, turning once, for 4 minutes, or just until golden brown. (Note: The chicken will not be cooked through and will finish in the oven.) Transfer the chicken to the sheet pan. Wipe out the skillet, add the remaining 1 tablespoon oil, and cook the second batch. Transfer to the sheet pan. Bake for 5 to 10 minutes, or until a thermometer inserted in the thickest portion registers 165°F and the juices run clear.

(CONTINUED)

✓ Crispy Parmesan Potato Wedges (recipe available on Thriving Home)

✓ Cranberry Spinach Salad with Creamy Citrus Vinaigrette (recipe available on Thriving Home)

✓ Cheesy Pesto Bread (recipe available on Thriving Home)

5. Meanwhile, wipe out the skillet with a paper towel. Over medium heat, melt 2 tablespoons of the butter (be careful not to burn the butter). Add the lemon juice, wine, the reserved lemon halves, $\frac{1}{2}$ teaspoon salt, and $\frac{1}{4}$ teaspoon pepper. Increase the heat to medium high and simmer, whisking constantly, until the sauce is reduced by half, about 2 minutes. Off the heat, add the remaining 4 tablespoons butter and swirl to combine. Stir in the fresh parsley. Taste and adjust the seasoning, if needed.

6. Discard the lemon halves and serve 1 piece of chicken on each plate. Spoon on the sauce and serve with a slice of lemon and a sprinkling of fresh parsley.

Freezer Meal Instructions

TO FREEZE: After completing Steps 2 and 3, place the breaded chicken in a gallon-size freezer bag or container in single layers, using parchment paper between layers so the chicken doesn't stick together. Then make the sauce, following the directions in Step 5. Once the sauce has cooled, pour it into a small freezer container or bag, and place with the chicken in the freezer.

TO PREPARE FROM FROZEN: Let the chicken and sauce thaw in the refrigerator overnight. Cook the chicken starting with Step 4. Warm the sauce on the stove in a pan over low heat or in the microwave, just until warm. Serve as suggested.

JANNY'S ROASTED CHICKEN

Sometimes the simplest recipes are the best. Take my mom's roasted chicken, for example. This classic recipe that I have grown up on has only four seasonings. This magic combination has a deep, savory flavor that tastes as good as it smells. It is incredibly easy to make and a crowd-pleaser. Get your money's worth out of this meal, too, by using leftovers for chicken sandwiches or on top of a salad the next day, and then making homemade Chicken Broth (page 217) with the bones! —POLLY *Yield: 6 servings*

1 teaspoon garlic salt

1 teaspoon onion salt

1 teaspoon celery salt

½ teaspoon ground savory

1 skin-on whole chicken (3–4 pounds), cut up into 6 pieces (If you can't find a whole chicken cut up at your grocery store, simply ask the butcher to do it for you. Otherwise, just use any combination of breasts, drumsticks, thighs, and wings.)

GOES WELL WITH

✓ Super Stuffed Baked Potatoes (page 121)

✓ Bread Machine Wheat Rolls (recipe available on Thriving Home)

✓ Basic Roasted Vegetables (recipe available on Thriving Home)

1. Preheat the oven to 350°F. Line a rimmed sheet pan with foil.

2. In a large bowl, mix together the garlic salt, onion salt, celery salt, and savory. Add the chicken pieces to the bowl and toss with the seasoning mix until well coated. *(Freezing directions begin here.)*

3. Place the chicken on the sheet pan, putting the smaller pieces toward the middle of the pan and the larger ones around the edges. Lay a piece of foil loosely over the top and bake for 25 minutes. Remove the foil and continue to bake for another 25 minutes, or until a thermometer inserted in the thickest portion registers 165°F and the juices run clear. If you want the skin to crisp up, broil the chicken for about 5 minutes at the very end.

4. Let the chicken rest for 5 to 10 minutes before serving.

Freezer Meal Instructions

TO FREEZE: Complete Step 2. Do not bake. Place the seasoned chicken in an airtight freezer container or gallon-size bag and freeze.

TO PREPARE FROM FROZEN: Let the chicken thaw in the refrigerator for 24 hours. Bake as directed.

GRILLED HONEY DIJON CHICKEN SANDWICHES

It's a good thing that my kids don't know what "Dijon" refers to, because their self-proclaimed mustard aversion might have caused them to miss out on this yummy sandwich. I was almost sure they would sniff it out and push the plate away, but, in reality, the opposite happened. Everyone in our family loved them! The sweetness of the honey is balanced with the zip of the Dijon mustard, resulting in a stellar marinated chicken breast that's even better when topped with cheese and bacon, and served in a bun. —POLLY Yield: 6 sandwiches

½ cup Dijon mustard

½ cup honey

Juice of half a lemon (1–2 tablespoons)

½ teaspoon paprika

½ teaspoon salt

½ teaspoon dried thyme

⅛ teaspoon red-pepper flakes (optional)

3 boneless, skinless chicken breasts, trimmed of fat

6 whole wheat hamburger buns

6 slices Swiss cheese

6 slices bacon, cooked

Lettuce and tomato slices (optional)

1. In a large mixing bowl, combine the mustard and honey. Add the lemon juice, paprika, salt, thyme, and red-pepper flakes (if using). Stir to combine.

2. Cut the chicken breasts in half horizontally. To do this, place your palm firmly on top of the chicken breast and slice with a sawing motion in half using a very sharp knife. You should now have 6 thin pieces of chicken breast.

3. Add the chicken to the marinade and turn to coat. *(Freezing instructions begin here.)* Cover and marinate in the refrigerator for at least an hour and up to 24 hours.

4. Remove the chicken to a plate and pour the marinade into a small saucepan. Bring to a boil over medium-high heat and cook for 3 to 5 minutes. Remove from the heat and set aside.

5. Preheat a grill or nonstick grill pan to medium heat (400–450°F). Cook the chicken, turning once, for about 8 minutes, or until a thermometer inserted in the thickest portion registers 165°F and the juices run clear.

6. On the bottom half of each bun, place a piece of chicken, a slice of cheese, a slice of bacon, a drizzle of the cooked marinade, and lettuce and tomato, if using.

(CONTINUED)

GOES WELL WITH

✓ Oven Fries with a
  Secret Ingredient
  (recipe available on
  Thriving Home)

✓ Coleslaw

Freezer Meal Instructions

TO FREEZE: Pour the marinade and chicken into a gallon-size freezer bag, seal, squeeze out any extra air, and freeze. Wrap the cheese and bacon in a layer of foil and freeze in a gallon-size freezer bag with the buns. Freeze next to the chicken.

TO PREPARE FROM FROZEN: Let the chicken and sandwich ingredients thaw in the refrigerator for 24 hours. Follow the cooking instructions beginning with Step 4.

Cooking Notes

▶ For some extra flavor, use the bacon grease to cook the chicken in a skillet.

INDIVIDUAL CHICKEN POT PIES

Recipe courtesy of Ann Timm from Keeper of the Home

Passed down through the generations, this recipe reminds me of the warmth of my Aunt Bubbie's kitchen and the way her homemade biscuits smelled as they steamed from the middle of the table. These individual pot pies are the kind of comfort food that makes memories deep in the heart. My great-grandmother cooked by adding a bit of this and some of that. According to my grandmother, it took some time to figure out just the right amounts to re-create her Granny Fontaine's dishes. Her chicken pot pies are still in high demand with all six of my kiddos. I hope they warm your hearts and bellies as they have ours! —ANN TIMM

Yield: 12 (3½") ramekins or jumbo muffin cups

¼ cup butter

1 small onion, chopped

¼ cup flour of your choice (Rachel and Polly prefer white whole wheat)

3 cups store-bought or homemade Chicken Broth (page 217)

3 carrots, sliced ¼" thick

¼ pound red potatoes, quartered and cut into ½" pieces

2 ribs celery, sliced ¼" thick

2½ cups diced cooked chicken

¼ teaspoon dried thyme

¼ teaspoon ground nutmeg

½ cup finely chopped fresh parsley or 4 teaspoons dried

Salt and ground black pepper

1 recipe Bubbie's Biscuits (recipe follows) or your preferred topping

1. Grease 12 ramekins or jumbo muffin cups generously with butter or olive oil.

2. In a large pot, melt the butter over medium heat. Cook the onion until tender, about 5 minutes. Add the flour and cook for about 1 minute, stirring constantly. Slowly whisk in the chicken broth until smooth.

3. Stir in the carrots, potatoes, and celery. Bring to a boil and simmer, stirring occasionally, until tender, about 10 minutes.

4. Add the chicken, thyme, nutmeg, parsley, and salt and pepper to taste. Gently stir to combine. Carefully ladle ½ cup of the mixture into each ramekin or muffin cup. Let stand for at least 1 hour (on the counter) or longer in the refrigerator (up to 24 hours) before baking. *(Freezing instructions begin here.)*

5. If making the biscuit recipe below, prepare it while the filling cools. Uncooked biscuits can be covered and refrigerated on a greased baking sheet until ready to use.

6. Preheat the oven to 450°F. Top each pot pie with 1 biscuit and place on a foil-lined baking sheet (to catch any overflow). Bake for 15 minutes, or until the biscuits are browned and the filling is bubbly.

(CONTINUED)

2 cups unbleached all-purpose flour

4 teaspoons baking powder

½ teaspoon baking soda

½ teaspoon salt

½ cup cold butter, cubed

1 cup buttermilk

BUBBIE'S BISCUITS

1. In a mixing bowl, sift together the flour, baking powder, baking soda, and salt.

2. Add the cold butter and cut in with a pastry blender or fork until the butter is the size of rice. Stir in the buttermilk until combined, but do not overmix.

3. Flour a clean surface. Dump out the dough, knead it a few times, and then roll it out until ½″ thick. Do not overhandle the dough, or it will become tough. Cut out biscuits with a biscuit cutter or upside-down glass. *(Freezing instructions begin here.)*

4. Place on top of the ready-to-bake chicken pot pies and follow recipe directions. Or bake on their own on a greased baking sheet at 475°F for about 10 minutes, or until lightly browned on top.

Freezer Meal Instructions

TO FREEZE

FILLING: Complete Step 4. Freeze until solid, 1 to 2 hours. Pop out of the ramekins or muffin pans and freeze individual portions in a freezer bag or container, sealing well.

BISCUITS: If making ahead, dust individual unbaked biscuits with flour and freeze in single layers divided by parchment paper in a gallon-size freezer bag alongside pot pies.

TO PREPARE FROM FROZEN

FILLING: Put frozen pot pies back into ramekins or muffin cups and thaw in the refrigerator overnight or on the counter for 1 hour before baking.

BISCUITS: Place on a greased baking sheet, cover, and let thaw in the refrigerator or on the counter if using right away.

Place a biscuit on top of each pot pie and bake according to the recipe directions.

CHEESY CHICKEN AND STUFFING CASSEROLE

The first meal I ever made for my husband when we were dating was a version of this very casserole. Maybe Cheesy Chicken and Stuffing Casserole can be classified as a "win your boyfriend's heart" tactic, because it sure worked. We've been happily married for 16 years now, and it still ranks among his favorite meals. The homemade cream of chicken soup and stuffing are *so* worth the extra time and effort. Their flavor is unlike anything you'll find at the store, plus you'll know exactly what is going into this comforting, crowd-pleaser. Make them in advance for an easy throw-together meal. —RACHEL Yield: 8 servings

2½ pounds chicken breasts, cut into 1" pieces

1 cup Cream of Chicken Soup (page 216)

2 cups shredded Cheddar cheese

3–3½ cups Simple Homemade Stuffing (recipe follows)

1. Preheat the oven to 350°F. Coat a 13" x 9" casserole dish with cooking spray. Pat the chicken very dry with paper towels.

2. Spread the chicken in the dish. Top with the cream of chicken soup, using a spatula or spoon to spread it evenly over the chicken. Sprinkle the cheese over the soup layer. Spread the prepared stuffing over the entire casserole. (*Freezing instructions begin here.*)

3. Bake for 40 to 45 minutes, or until the sides are bubbling and the top is golden brown.

Freezer Meal Instructions

TO FREEZE: Cover the dish tightly with several layers of plastic wrap and 1 or 2 layers of foil (or an airtight lid), squeeze out excess air, and freeze.

TO PREPARE FROM FROZEN: Thaw completely in the refrigerator. Set out on the counter for about 30 minutes before baking to bring the casserole up to room temperature. Bake according to recipe directions.

4 cups cubed (about ¼") whole grain bread pieces

¼ cup butter

1 tablespoon dried onion flakes or 1 teaspoon onion powder

¼ teaspoon garlic powder

½ teaspoon celery seed

1 tablespoon dried parsley, crushed in hand

½ teaspoon ground sage

½ teaspoon ground thyme

½ teaspoon salt

¼ teaspoon ground black pepper

1½ cups store-bought or homemade Chicken Broth (page 217)

GOES WELL WITH

✓ Homemade Wheat Sandwich Bread (recipe available on Thriving Home)

✓ A simple green salad with Balsamic Parmesan Salad Dressing (recipe available on Thriving Home)

SIMPLE HOMEMADE STUFFING

1. Preheat the oven to 350°F.

2. Spread the bread pieces on a rimmed baking sheet and bake for 8 to 10 minutes. Using a spatula, stir the bread and spread it back out again. Bake for 6 to 8 minutes, or until the bread is completely toasted. Set aside.

3. In a 2-quart pot, melt the butter over medium heat (do not let the butter brown). Stir in the onion flakes or powder, garlic powder, celery seed, parsley, sage, thyme, salt, pepper, and chicken broth. Increase the heat to high and bring to a boil.

4. Once boiling, remove the pot from the heat. Quickly add the toasted bread pieces and gently stir to coat evenly. Place a tight-fitting lid on top of the pot. Let sit for 5 to 7 minutes, covered, or until most of the liquid is absorbed.

5. Use a fork to gently fluff the stuffing before serving or using in the casserole recipe. Store in an airtight container in the refrigerator for up to 3 days or in the freezer for up to 1 month.

Cooking Notes

▶ Don't throw away old bread! Store it in a freezer bag in the freezer until you're ready to make the stuffing.

▶ This casserole is a great way to use up leftover stuffing or precooked chicken or turkey. If using precooked poultry, reduce the baking time to about 30 minutes, or until the casserole is warmed through and golden on top.

▶ Try adding cooked broccoli pieces to the casserole to add more nutrition. Layer the cooked broccoli after the chicken and before the cream of chicken soup.

SHEET PAN LEMON-GARLIC CHICKEN AND VEGGIES

I told my husband recently, "I could eat my weight in roasted vegetables." There is no better way to cook them, if you're asking this girl. I especially enjoy the bright hint of lemon from the marinade in both the chicken and broccoli/carrot/cauliflower mix in this particular recipe. Toss the veggies with a little fresh Parmesan at the end, and you won't be disappointed. Bonus: The leftovers are just as delicious the next day. —RACHEL *Yield: 4–5 servings*

6 tablespoons olive oil

Zest of 1 lemon

Juice of 1 lemon (about 2 tablespoons)

4 cloves garlic, minced

1 teaspoon salt

½ teaspoon ground black pepper

1 teaspoon minced fresh thyme leaves or ¼ teaspoon dried

1½ pounds boneless, skinless chicken breasts, trimmed of any visible fat

1 bag (12 ounces) fresh chopped broccoli, petite carrots, and cauliflower blend (or 12 ounces of any of these vegetables)

Grated Parmesan cheese

1. In a large resealable freezer bag, combine the olive oil, lemon zest and juice, garlic, salt, pepper, and thyme. Seal and shake to mix. Add the chicken, seal, and toss to coat. (*Freezing instructions begin here.*) Marinate in the refrigerator for 1 hour or up to 24 hours.

2. Place a rack in the middle of the oven and preheat the oven to 400°F. Place a rimmed sheet pan in the oven while it's preheating.

3. Carefully remove the hot sheet pan and coat it with cooking spray. Using tongs, remove the chicken from the marinade, shaking off any extra marinade inside the bag. (Reserve the marinade.) Place the chicken breasts in the middle of the pan, making sure they don't touch. Roast on the middle rack for about 20 minutes, turning once, or until a thermometer inserted in the thickest portion registers 165°F and the juices run clear.

4. Set the chicken aside on a serving platter and cover with foil to keep warm. Increase the oven temperature to 425°F. Generously coat the same sheet pan with cooking spray.

5. Add the vegetables to the marinade bag, seal, and toss to coat. Spread the vegetables evenly around the sheet, making sure they don't touch. Roast for about 20 minutes, turning once, or until crisp. Toss with the cheese.

6. Arrange the roasted vegetables on the platter with the chicken and serve.

(CONTINUED)

✓ Brown rice or quinoa

✓ Warm whole grain bread with butter and honey

✓ Fruit slices, like apples or pears

Freezer Meal Instructions

TO FREEZE: Mix the marinade in a gallon-size freezer bag. Add the chicken, seal, and shake to coat. Freeze.

TO PREPARE FROM FROZEN: Thaw the chicken in the refrigerator for about 24 hours. Follow the preheating and cooking instructions in the recipe above, beginning with Step 2.

Cooking Notes

▶ Switch out the broccoli/carrots/cauliflower medley for your favorite vegetables. Some ideas: Brussels sprouts, green beans, sweet potatoes, or baby gold potatoes.

▶ If you have a second oven, keep the chicken in there at 200°F to stay warm.

CHICKEN FRIED RICE
WITH MAPLE SOY SAUCE

A version of this fried rice has been in our menu rotation for years. But after testing this particular recipe, I texted Polly, "I want to face-plant into this pan of fried rice!" Not only does it taste ah-mazing, but as busy moms, we love one-dish wonders that can use up leftovers and clean out the fridge. Plus, picky kids and adults go for the bounty of finely chopped veggies in this one because of the salty-sweet sauce that coats (and camouflages) all the nutritious ingredients. Leftovers are even better the next day. —RACHEL Yield: 4–6 servings

Olive oil or avocado oil

½ pound boneless, skinless chicken breasts, diced

Salt and ground black pepper

3 eggs, lightly beaten

¾ cup finely chopped broccoli

¾ cup finely chopped carrot (about 1 large carrot)

2 cloves garlic, minced

½ cup frozen peas

¼ cup sliced scallions or chopped fresh chives

4 cups cooked brown rice

Maple Soy Sauce (recipe follows)

1. In a large skillet or wok, heat 1 tablespoon oil over medium-high heat. Season chicken lightly on all sides with salt and pepper to taste. Stir-fry the chicken until no longer pink and the juices run clear, about 4 minutes. Remove chicken and set aside.

2. Add more oil to the pan, if needed. Pour the eggs into the pan. Cook, stirring occasionally, for 1 to 2 minutes, or until set. Remove the eggs from the pan and set aside.

3. Wipe the pan out, if needed. Add 1 tablespoon oil to the pan. Add the broccoli, carrot, and garlic and season to taste with salt and pepper. Stir-fry for 4 minutes, or until tender. Add the peas and scallions or chives and stir-fry for 1 minute.

4. Add the rice to the pan. Stir-fry for about 3 minutes, or until heated through. Stir in the reserved chicken and eggs. Drizzle with the Maple Soy Sauce and toss to combine. *(Freezing instructions begin here.)*

(CONTINUED)

¼ cup naturally brewed tamari soy sauce (recommended: Kikkoman brand)

3 tablespoons pure maple syrup

2 tablespoons unsalted butter

1 tablespoon dried onion flakes

⅛ teaspoon red-pepper flakes (optional; can add more to taste)

GOES WELL WITH
✓ Shrimp Pot Stickers (page 138)

MAPLE SOY SAUCE

In a small saucepan, bring the soy sauce, maple syrup, butter, onion, and red-pepper flakes (if using) to a boil. Reduce the heat and simmer for 2 minutes.

Freezer Meal Instructions

TO FREEZE: Prepare as directed, fully cool, and then freeze flat in a gallon-size freezer bag.

TO PREPARE FROM FROZEN: Thaw in the refrigerator overnight or place in a microwave-safe bowl and thaw in the microwave using the defrost setting. Warm gently in the microwave or in a skillet over low heat, stirring occasionally.

Family Favorite Baked
Meatballs, *page 96*

CHAPTER 6
beef

FAMILY FAVORITE BAKED MEATBALLS

These baked meatballs are super tender and tasty and have become my go-to "baby meal" to take to friends with newborns. I pack them up along with a box of whole grain spaghetti, some marinara sauce, a salad or veggie tray, and some chopped-up fruit. I always, always double this recipe so I can have extra on hand for our family or friends in need. By baking the meatballs on a rack, the fat drips below, which results in less greasy meatballs. To make this recipe gluten-free, simply substitute almond meal or gluten-free bread crumbs for the whole wheat bread crumbs. —RACHEL Yield: about 24 (1½") meatballs

1½ pounds lean ground beef

½ cup dried whole wheat bread crumbs (or whole wheat panko bread crumbs)

½ cup freshly grated Parmesan cheese

½ cup packed fresh parsley, finely chopped

2–3 leaves fresh basil, finely chopped

1 large egg, beaten

2 tablespoons milk

2 tablespoons tomato paste

½ teaspoon salt

½ teaspoon ground black pepper

½ teaspoon garlic powder

½ teaspoon dried oregano, crushed in hand

4 cups Slow Cooker Marinara Sauce (page 212), for serving (optional)

1. Preheat the oven to 350°F. Line a rimmed sheet pan with parchment paper or foil; place an oven-safe rack on top of the pan, if using.

2. In a medium bowl, using your hands, gently combine the ground beef, bread crumbs, cheese, parsley, basil, egg, milk, tomato paste, salt, pepper, garlic powder, and oregano. Do not overmix.

3. Use a medium dough scooper or a spoon to scoop and roll about 1½" meatballs. Line up the meatballs on the sheet pan or on the rack, leaving room between each. *(Freezing instructions for Method 1 begin here.)*

4. Bake for 20 minutes, or until no longer pink. *(Freezing instructions for Method 2 begin here.)*

5. Serve with marinara sauce alone, on top of pasta, or on a sandwich.

Freezer Meal Instructions

TO FREEZE

METHOD 1: UNCOOKED MEATBALLS: Flash freeze uncooked meatballs by placing the pan in the freezer for about an hour or so. Once frozen, dump meatballs in a gallon-size freezer bag or container and freeze.

METHOD 2: COOKED MEATBALLS IN SAUCE: Fully cook and cool the meatballs. Combine with marinara sauce and freeze in a freezer bag or container.

✓ Bread Machine Wheat Rolls (recipe available on Thriving Home)

✓ Roasted Brussels Sprouts with Bacon & Honey Balsamic Reduction (recipe available on Thriving Home)

✓ A salad with Honey Dijon Vinaigrette Salad Dressing (recipe available on Thriving Home)

TO PREPARE FROM FROZEN

METHOD 1: UNCOOKED MEATBALLS: Thaw meatballs in the refrigerator overnight (preferred method) or using the cool water method (submerge the freezer bag in cold water until thawed, replacing the water every 30 minutes). Cook according to recipe instructions.

METHOD 2: COOKED MEATBALLS IN SAUCE: Thaw meatballs and sauce in the refrigerator overnight (preferred method) or using the cool water method (submerge the freezer bag in cold water until thawed, replacing the water every 30 minutes). Warm gently in marinara sauce on the stovetop or in a slow cooker.

CHEDDAR CHIVE BURGERS

There's nothing quite like a big juicy homemade burger, eh? And if you're going to the trouble of making a few, why not double or triple the recipe to have more on hand for anytime? These moist, cheesy burgers freeze well and thaw overnight in the fridge. The fresh herbs and shredded cheese inside the burgers take these patties over the top in taste, plus add a bit of sneaky greens inside, too. Yield: 6 burgers

⅓ cup finely chopped fresh parsley

3 tablespoons minced fresh chives

4 large cloves garlic, minced

1¼ teaspoons salt

½ teaspoon ground black pepper

1½ cups shredded sharp Cheddar cheese

2 pounds ground beef (recommended: 80% lean)

6 slices Cheddar cheese (optional)

6 whole grain buns, toasted, or 6 large lettuce leaves

GOES WELL WITH

✓ Oven Fries with a Secret Ingredient (recipe available on Thriving Home)

✓ Corn on the cob

✓ Veggie sticks and hummus

1. In a large bowl, combine the parsley, chives, garlic, salt, pepper, and shredded cheese. Add the ground beef and use your hands to combine gently. Do not overmix. Divide mixture into 6 equal portions and form burger patties. Make a slight indentation in the middle of the burger so that the edges are thicker. (*Freezing instructions begin here.*)

2. On a preheated grill or in a grill pan over high heat (about 450°F), cook the burgers for 4 minutes, turning once, or until golden brown. Do not push down on the burgers while they cook. Move to a cooler area of the grill or reduce the heat under the grill pan and cook to the desired doneness, another 3 to 4 minutes (for medium) or 5 to 6 minutes (for well-done). A well-done burger is no longer pink inside and has an internal temperature of 165°F. During the last minute of cooking, add the cheese slices on top, if using.

3. Serve on the whole grain buns or large lettuce leaves with your favorite toppings and condiments.

Freezer Meal Instructions

TO FREEZE: Package uncooked patties in single layers between pieces of parchment or waxed paper in a freezer bag and freeze.

TO PREPARE FROM FROZEN: Thaw completely in the refrigerator, about 24 hours. Set on the counter and bring up to room temperature for 20 to 30 minutes. Follow the cooking instructions above.

GRILLED FLANK STEAK
WITH CHIMICHURRI SAUCE

Flank steak is a fabulous grilling steak. If handled just right, this lean cut works great for carne asada, steak tacos, fajitas, or on its own with just the classic seasonings: kosher salt and freshly ground black pepper. For our recipe, a smoky rub transforms this humble piece of meat and is complemented by a zesty chimichurri sauce for the ultimate finish. It's hard to believe that this colorful, fresh meal also works well as a freezer meal. Yield: 6 servings

CHIMICHURRI SAUCE

⅔ cup loosely packed fresh parsley

⅔ cup loosely packed cilantro

4 cloves garlic

¼ cup chopped red onion

¼ cup apple cider vinegar

1 teaspoon salt

¼ teaspoon red-pepper flakes

¼ teaspoon ground black pepper

½ cup extra-virgin olive oil

STEAK RUB

1 teaspoon garlic powder

1 teaspoon ground cumin

1 teaspoon dried oregano

1 teaspoon salt

½ teaspoon ground black pepper

2 pounds flank steak

1. Preheat the grill or a grill pan to high heat (450°F).

2. *To make the chimichurri sauce:* In a food processor, combine the parsley, cilantro, garlic, onion, vinegar, salt, red-pepper flakes, and black pepper. Process until smooth. While pulsing the food processor, drizzle in the olive oil until the sauce is well combined. Set aside.

3. *To make the rub:* In a small bowl, combine the garlic powder, cumin, oregano, salt, and black pepper. Rub the seasoning into the surface of the steak on all sides. *(Freezing instructions begin here.)*

4. Grill the steak over direct heat for 2 to 3 minutes. Rotate it 45 degrees. Grill for 2 to 3 minutes more, and then turn to cook the other side. Cook for 2 to 3 minutes, rotate the steak 45 degrees, and cook for 2 to 3 minutes more, or until a thermometer inserted in the center registers 145°F for medium-rare or 160°F for medium. Do not overcook.

5. Let the steak rest for 5 to 8 minutes. Slice thinly across the grain. Top the steak with a drizzle of the chimichurri sauce.

Freezer Meal Instructions

TO FREEZE

CHIMICHURRI SAUCE: Puree all of the chimichurri ingredients in the food processor, except for the vinegar. Place the chimichurri in a freezer container or bag, squeezing out all of the air before sealing. Place the vinegar in a separate small freezer bag or container and freeze alongside the chimichurri. (*Note:* The vinegar will cause the ingredients to brown if frozen and thawed together.)

(CONTINUED)

STEAK: After seasoning the steak in Step 3, wrap it in plastic wrap and then place it in an airtight freezer bag, squeezing out all of the air before sealing.

TO PREPARE FROM FROZEN

Thaw all of the ingredients in the refrigerator for 24 hours. Before serving, set the chimichurri on the counter, stir in the vinegar, and let the sauce come up to room temperature. Grill the steak as instructed and serve with the chimichurri sauce.

Cooking Notes

▶ Chimichurri sauce is best when served at room temperature.

▶ The key to a great flank steak is grilling it medium-rare to medium.

EASY BEEFY QUESADILLAS

After a long day and with a kitchen full of little people, I didn't have the focus or the luxury of much time to make an elaborate dinner. I wanted something that pleased everyone's palate and was quick and easy to whip up. Since quesadillas are always a top choice for my kids, I figured I would try stuffing them with a tasty beef and bean mixture instead of just plain ole cheese, as usual. To add some extra nutrition, you could add some sautéed green and red peppers, too. The result was a (rare) huge success in our home of fickle taste testers. —POLLY

Yield: 8 quesadillas

2 tablespoons olive oil or avocado oil

½ medium white onion, diced

1 pound lean ground beef

2 teaspoons ground cumin

1 teaspoon salt

½ cup frozen or canned corn

½ cup black beans, rinsed and drained

1 cup salsa

2 tablespoons butter

16 whole wheat tortillas (8" diameter)

2 cups shredded Cheddar cheese

1. In a large nonstick skillet, heat the oil over medium heat. Cook the onion, stirring frequently, until it begins to soften, 4 to 5 minutes. Add the ground beef, cumin, and salt. Cook until the beef is no longer pink. Drain.

2. Reduce the heat to low and stir in the corn, black beans, and salsa. Cook for 2 to 3 minutes, stirring occasionally. Set aside. (*Freezing instructions begin here.*)

3. In another large skillet or a griddle, melt a small amount of the butter over medium-low heat.

4. Place a tortilla in the skillet and spread about 2 tablespoons of cheese and a heaping ½ cup of the beef mixture over it. Top the beef with another 2 tablespoons of cheese and then another tortilla.

5. Cook for 4 to 6 minutes, turning once, until the tortilla is browned and a bit firm. Before turning, be sure to add butter to the other side of the quesadilla! Repeat to make 8 quesadillas.

6. Serve warm and cut into triangles. Top with guacamole, salsa, or sour cream.

(CONTINUED)

✓ Avocado Lime Salsa
  (recipe available on
  Thriving Home)

✓ Creamy Avocado
  Dip (recipe
  available on
  Thriving Home)

Freezer Meal Instructions

TO FREEZE: Place cooked and cooled beef filling in an airtight freezer bag or container. In a separate bag, freeze the cheese. In yet another bag, freeze the tortillas. Freeze all the bags together as a kit.

TO PREPARE FROM FROZEN: Let all ingredients thaw in the refrigerator overnight. Follow the cooking instructions as directed, beginning in Step 3.

Cooking Notes

▶ If you want to, you could assemble the quesadillas and freeze them before cooking. This method makes the preparation go a bit faster, but it can be tricky, as the contents could easily spill out while transferring.

BEEF AND BEAN BURRITOS

If you're cooking for only one or two people or you need a new lunch box option, you'll want to stock your freezer with these burritos. Not only can they be frozen individually, but they're also budget-friendly, packed with nutritious ingredients, and quite filling. Because half of the beans are mashed before they're added in, each bite is creamy and easy to eat on the go. The ground beef filling is far from bland, seasoned with bold flavors like cumin, chili powder, tomato paste, and lime juice. Use fresh toppings like sour cream, guacamole, or salsa to complete the dish. Yield: 10 burritos

---

3 cups store-bought or homemade Chicken Broth (page 217), divided

8 cloves garlic, minced, divided

1½ cups instant whole grain brown rice

⅓ cup minced fresh cilantro

1 can (15 ounces) pinto beans, rinsed and drained, divided

1 tablespoon olive oil or avocado oil

1 onion, diced

1 green bell pepper, diced

¼ cup tomato paste

1 tablespoon ground cumin

1 teaspoon dried oregano

1 teaspoon chili powder

1 pound lean ground beef

1 tablespoon lime juice

4 cups shredded sharp Cheddar cheese

10 whole wheat tortillas (10" diameter)

Sour cream, guacamole, and salsa for serving

1. Preheat the oven to 400°F. Line a baking sheet with foil (to make for easy cleanup).

2. In a large pot over medium-high heat, bring 2½ cups of the chicken broth and half of the garlic to a boil. Add the rice and cook according to package directions. Allow the rice to cool for 10 to 15 minutes, fluff with a fork, and stir in the cilantro. Set aside.

3. In a small mixing bowl, combine half of the beans and the remaining ½ cup chicken broth. Using a potato masher or the flat bottom side of a fork, mash until the beans no longer have large clumps. Set aside.

4. In a large nonstick skillet, heat the oil over medium heat. Add the onion and bell pepper and cook until they begin to soften, about 5 minutes. Stir in the remaining garlic, the tomato paste, cumin, oregano, and chili powder.

5. Increase the heat to medium high. Add the ground beef and cook, breaking up the meat, until it's no longer pink, about 5 minutes. Stir in the remaining beans, the reserved mashed bean mixture, and the lime juice. Remove from the heat.

GOES WELL WITH

✓ Avocado Lime Salsa
  (recipe available on
  Thriving Home)

✓ Roasted Corn and
  Black Bean Salsa
  (recipe available on
  Thriving Home)

✓ Tortilla chips

6. To assemble your burritos, start by sprinkling $1/3$ cup shredded cheese over each tortilla. Add a scant $1/3$ cup of rice followed by a heaping $1/3$ cup of beef mixture.

7. Fold the sides of each tortilla over the filling. Then fold the bottom of the tortilla over the sides and filling. Roll the burrito tightly and place seam side down on the baking sheet. *(Freezing instructions begin here.)*

8. Sprinkle the tops of the burritos with the remaining cheese and bake for 10 to 15 minutes, or until the cheese has melted. Serve with favorite toppings.

Freezer Meal Instructions

TO FREEZE: After assembling the burritos in Step 7, wrap each uncooked burrito in foil. Place wrapped burritos in a gallon-size freezer bag, seal, and freeze.

TO PREPARE FROM FROZEN

OVEN METHOD: Unwrap foil from burritos and place on a foil-lined baking sheet. Sprinkle with cheese, and bake at 400°F for 10 to 15 minutes.

MICROWAVE METHOD: Remove foil. Defrost in the microwave using the defrost setting for about 5 minutes. Top burritos with cheese and microwave on high power for 1 minute.

TOTALLY TASTY TACO KIT

The taco dinner kits from the store are convenient but lack freshness and flavor. Instead of spending money on a preservative-filled, dull taco dinner, make an even better-tasting one at home! Freeze the seasoned cooked meat, along with tortillas and freshly shredded cheese, for a super easy meal to dish out for lunch or dinner as needed. Everyone can add their favorite fresh toppings, like lettuce, tomatoes, or sour cream, to personalize their tacos.

Yield: 8 tacos

2 tablespoons chili powder

1 teaspoon ground cumin

1 teaspoon ground coriander

½ teaspoon dried oregano

¼ teaspoon ground cayenne pepper

1 teaspoon salt

½ teaspoon ground black pepper

2 tablespoons olive oil or avocado oil

½ large yellow onion, finely chopped

3 cloves garlic, minced

1 pound lean ground beef or lean ground turkey

¾ cup store-bought or homemade Chicken Broth (page 217)

8 whole wheat tortillas (8" diameter)

Shredded Cheddar cheese, guacamole, salsa, sour cream, lettuce, etc. (optional, for serving)

1. In a small bowl, combine the chili powder, cumin, coriander, oregano, cayenne pepper, salt, and black pepper. Set aside.

2. In a large skillet, heat the oil over medium heat. Cook the onion, stirring frequently, until softened, 4 to 5 minutes. Stir in the garlic and cook for 30 to 60 seconds more.

3. Increase the heat to medium high. Add the ground beef and cook for 5 minutes, or until no longer pink, breaking up the meat with a wooden spoon as it browns. Drain off excess grease.

4. Sprinkle the reserved spice mixture over the meat and stir until coated. Add in the broth and bring to a boil. Reduce the heat to medium low and simmer, uncovered, until the mixture has thickened, 4 to 5 minutes. (*Freezing instructions begin here.*)

5. Warm the tortillas according to package directions.

6. Serve the warm meat mixture on the tortillas with desired toppings.

Freezer Meal Instructions

TO FREEZE: Cook the meat as directed, then let the mixture cool completely. Place it in a freezer container or bag, seal well, and freeze. In separate freezer containers or bags, freeze about 1 cup of shredded cheese and 8 tortillas, along with the meat, to complete your kit.

TO PREPARE FROM FROZEN: Let all ingredients thaw in the refrigerator. Serve as directed.

(THE ONLY) SLOPPY JOES (WE LIKE)

After polling dozens of my friends and family, I learned that Sloppy Joes are quite the divisive meal. People either love them or hate them. I counted myself as a hater until just a few years ago because I always envisioned the canned version from childhood. Yuck! But I was won over by this particular recipe; the tangy-sweet tomato sauce surprised me in a good way. Now these are the only Sloppy Joes my family (and Polly's family, too) likes! —RACHEL

Yield: 4 generous servings

---

4 whole wheat hamburger buns (or 8 mini buns)

3 teaspoons olive oil or avocado oil, divided

1 pound lean ground beef

2 teaspoons all-natural steak seasoning (Recommended: Weber Montana Steak Seasoning or Emeril's All-Natural Steak Rub)

2 tablespoons maple syrup, divided

½ medium onion, finely chopped

1 medium carrot, finely chopped or finely shredded

2 cloves garlic, minced

1 tablespoon apple cider vinegar or white vinegar

1 tablespoon Worcestershire sauce

2 cans (8 ounces each) unsalted tomato sauce

2 tablespoons tomato paste

Salt

Cheddar cheese slices (optional)

---

1. Preheat the broiler to high. Place the buns on a baking sheet with the insides facing up.

2. Meanwhile, in a large skillet, heat 1 teaspoon of the oil over medium-high heat. Add the ground beef and cook for 2 minutes, breaking it up with a spoon as it cooks. Add the steak seasoning and 1 tablespoon of the maple syrup and stir to combine with the meat. Cook until the meat is no longer pink, about 5 minutes, remove from the pan, and place on a plate lined with paper towels.

3. Wipe the skillet out. Heat the remaining 2 teaspoons oil over medium-high heat. Add the onion, carrot, garlic, vinegar, and Worcestershire. Cook until the veggies are tender, 4 to 5 minutes.

4. Add the cooked meat, tomato sauce, tomato paste, and remaining 1 tablespoon maple syrup to the skillet. Stir to combine. Reduce the heat to a simmer and cook the mixture for 5 minutes longer. Season with salt to taste, if needed. *(Freezing instructions begin here.)*

5. Broil the buns for 1 to 2 minutes, or until golden. Watch carefully so they do not burn.

6. Using a large spoon or ice cream scoop, pile the meat mixture onto the toasted bun bottoms. Add slices of cheese, if desired, and cover with the tops of the buns.

✓ Asian Slaw (recipe available on Thriving Home)

✓ Corn on the cob

✓ Watermelon slices

Freezer Meal Instructions

TO FREEZE: Fully cook and cool the Sloppy Joes mixture. Place in a gallon-size freezer bag or freezer-safe container, removing as much air as possible. Seal and freeze.

TO PREPARE FROM FROZEN: Thaw in the microwave using the defrost setting or for about 24 hours in the refrigerator. Then warm over low to medium-low heat in a pot on the stove, gently stirring. Assemble the Sloppy Joes as directed.

Cooking Notes

▶ Place the onion and carrot pieces in a food processor for easy fine chopping.

Foolproof Roasted Pork
Tenderloin, *page 114*

pork and turkey

FOOLPROOF ROASTED PORK TENDERLOIN

A s one of my Freezer Club's most popular freezer meals, this pork tenderloin was requested over and over through the years. It's surprisingly simple, unbelievably delicious, kid-friendly, cheap, and healthy—all my indicators of a perfect recipe. In fact, I often make this when guests come over or for holiday meals. It truly is foolproof. Don't forget to double, triple, or quadruple this one and freeze for another day. —RACHEL Yield: 4 servings

1 teaspoon garlic powder

1 teaspoon dried oregano

1 teaspoon ground cumin

1 teaspoon ground coriander

½ teaspoon ground thyme

1 teaspoon salt

1¼ pounds pork tenderloin, trimmed of fat and silver skin

1 tablespoon olive oil or avocado oil

GOES WELL WITH

✓ Cheesy Mashed Sweet Potatoes (recipe available on Thriving Home)

✓ Steamed green beans

1. Preheat the oven to 450°F. Coat a rimmed sheet pan with cooking spray or line with foil.

2. In a small bowl, combine the garlic powder, oregano, cumin, coriander, thyme, and salt. Pat the pork tenderloin dry with paper towels. Sprinkle the rub over the tenderloin with a dry hand, then rub the seasoning over all sides of the meat, pressing gently so the seasoning adheres well. *(Freezing instructions begin here.)*

3. In a large skillet, heat the oil over medium-high heat. Place the tenderloin in the pan and cook for about 5 minutes, using tongs to turn it and sear the meat on all sides.

4. Transfer the meat to the sheet pan and roast for about 20 minutes, or until a thermometer inserted in the center registers 145°F and the juices run clear. It will still be slightly pink inside. Let the meat rest for 5 to 10 minutes so the juices redistribute. Slice on an angle and serve.

Freezer Meal Instructions

TO FREEZE: Place the uncooked, seasoned pork tenderloin in a gallon-size freezer bag. Pressing all the air out, seal tightly and freeze.

TO PREPARE FROM FROZEN: Thaw the tenderloin in the refrigerator for about 24 hours. Start by following Step 3, searing the tenderloin, and then roasting it in the pre-heated oven according to the recipe instructions.

Cooking Notes

▶ A meat thermometer is essential to not overcooking pork tenderloin.

YUM LOAVES

After my third child was born, my friend Jessi was kind enough to bring us a meal. When she showed up at my door with "Ham Loaves," I was a bit skeptical. Ham loaves? Hmmm? However, all skepticism was cast aside after my first bite. This dish surprised me with its unique flavor. The sweet-savory glaze that was caramelized over the top was perfect with the flavors in the meat mixture. After I tweaked the original recipe to make it with whole food ingredients, my kids started calling them "Yum Loaves." The name stuck around, and so has the recipe. —POLLY Yield: 6 individual loaves

LOAVES

1 pound ground ham (If you can't find this item, ask for help at the butcher counter.)

1 pound ground pork

½ cup dried whole wheat bread crumbs

3 tablespoons finely chopped yellow onion

1 large egg, beaten

¾ cup whole milk

¼ teaspoon liquid smoke

BROWN SUGAR GLAZE

¾ cup brown sugar

1½ teaspoons dry mustard or 1½ tablespoons prepared mustard

¼ cup white vinegar

¼ teaspoon liquid smoke

1. *To make the loaves:* Preheat the oven to 350°F. Line a 13″ x 9″ glass or ceramic casserole dish with foil. Coat generously with cooking spray.

2. In a large mixing bowl, combine the ham, pork, bread crumbs, onion, egg, milk, and liquid smoke. Use your hands to mix together well.

3. Working with a half-cup portion at a time, shape the mixture into 6 individual loaves and place them in the baking dish, making sure they don't touch.

4. *To make the glaze:* In a small bowl, mix together the brown sugar, mustard, vinegar, and liquid smoke. Pour the glaze generously over the loaves. *(Freezing instructions begin here.)*

5. Bake the loaves for 1 hour and 15 minutes. Let cool slightly before serving.

Freezer Meal Instructions

TO FREEZE: Complete the Yum Loaves and glaze through Step 4, but do not bake. Seal the casserole dish with an airtight lid or wrap the dish with a few layers of plastic wrap and with a layer or two of foil. Freeze.

TO PREPARE FROM FROZEN: Let the loaves thaw in the fridge for 24 hours. Set the dish out on the counter for about 30 minutes before baking to bring the loaves to room temperature, and bake as directed.

FOUR-INGREDIENT SEASONED PORK CHOPS

We all need a few easy-peasy recipes to fall back on, and this one can be whipped up in under 20 minutes. These savory chops are loved by all ages, plus you probably have all the seasonings in your pantry. Searing the chops gives them a nice little crust that adds to the deliciousness. When pork chops are on sale, be sure to stock your freezer with them so you can throw this meal together when you need something last minute. To make the chops gluten-free, you could eliminate the flour from the seasoned rub. *Yield: 4 servings*

2 tablespoons whole wheat flour

1 teaspoon salt

1 teaspoon garlic salt

½ teaspoon ground black pepper

4 boneless pork chops (1½" thick)

1–2 tablespoons olive oil or avocado oil

GOES WELL WITH

✓ Super Stuffed Baked Potatoes (page 121)

✓ Oven-Roasted Broccoli (recipe available on Thriving Home)

1. In a small bowl, mix together the flour, salt, garlic salt, and pepper.

2. Lightly coat both sides of each pork chop with the rub. *(Freezing instructions begin here.)*

3. In a large nonstick skillet, heat the oil over medium-high heat. Place the pork chops in the pan and sear each side for 1 to 2 minutes. Be careful, as the oil may splatter. Use a lid if necessary. Reduce the heat to medium low and cook for 10 to 15 minutes, turning once, or until a thermometer inserted in the center of a chop registers 145°F and the juices run clear.

4. Let the pork chops rest for 5 to 10 minutes before serving.

Freezer Meal Instructions

TO FREEZE: Place the seasoned, uncooked pork chops in an airtight freezer container or bag, separating them with parchment paper, and freeze.

TO PREPARE FROM FROZEN: Thaw the pork chops in the refrigerator for 24 hours. Follow the cooking instructions.

SWEET AND SAVORY PORK CHOPS

I'll be honest. I spent *a lot* of time scouring different recipes and gathering intel on what makes for an outstanding pork chop. We found that this basic garlic, honey, and soy sauce marinade changed what can be a boring cut of meat into a sweet-savory delight. What really enhances these chops is reducing that same marinade into a delectable, sticky sauce to drizzle over the top just before eating. Keep in mind that boneless pork chops can easily overcook if you aren't careful. Using a meat thermometer is the key to getting them just right. —POLLY

Yield: 6 servings

½ cup soy sauce

½ cup honey

2 teaspoons minced garlic

1 teaspoon salt

6 boneless pork chops (1" thick)

1–2 tablespoons olive oil or avocado oil (for stovetop cooking)

1. In a small bowl, whisk together the soy sauce, honey, garlic, and salt. Place the marinade and pork chops in a gallon-size resealable bag. *(Freezing instructions begin here.)*

2. Allow the pork chops to marinate for at least 2 hours or up to 24 hours in the refrigerator. Cook the pork chops using a cooking method below.

COOKING METHOD #1, STOVETOP: In a large nonstick skillet, heat the oil over medium-high heat. Remove the pork chops from the marinade and place in the pan, but do not discard the marinade. Sear for 1 to 2 minutes per side, turning once. Reduce the heat to medium low and cook, turning once, for 10 to 15 minutes, or until a thermometer inserted in the center of a chop registers 145°F and the juices run clear. Remove from the heat and let the chops rest for 5 to 10 minutes.

COOKING METHOD #2, BAKING: Preheat the oven to 350°F. Line a rimmed sheet pan with foil and coat with cooking spray. Remove the pork chops from the marinade and place the pork on the pan, but do not discard the marinade. Bake for 30 to 35 minutes, or until a thermometer inserted in the center of a chop registers 145°F and the juices run clear.

3. Meanwhile, pour the remaining marinade in a small saucepan and bring it to a boil. Reduce the heat and simmer for about 3 minutes. Drizzle the cooked marinade over the pork and serve.

GOES WELL WITH

✓ Super Stuffed
  Baked Potatoes
  (page 121)

✓ Asian Slaw (recipe
  available on
  Thriving Home)

Freezer Meal Instructions

TO FREEZE: Instead of placing the marinating pork chops in the fridge, freeze them in a gallon-size freezer bag.

TO PREPARE FROM FROZEN: Let the pork chops and marinade thaw in the fridge for 24 hours. Prepare as directed.

Cooking Notes

▶ To kick up the flavor a notch, add $1/4$ teaspoon red-pepper flakes and/or $1/4$ teaspoon ground black pepper to the marinade.

▶ Some of our recipe testers had success with searing the pork chops for 1 to 2 minutes on each side and then baking them until done.

HAM AND SWISS GLAZED PANINIS

If I had to say which recipe in this book was my kids' favorite, it would be this one. They *loved* these sandwiches. So much so that I plan on doubling or even tripling this recipe anytime I make it in the future. What puts these paninis over the top is the brown sugar glaze—yep, I just said brown sugar glaze—that seeps into the bread and sweetens every bite. Plus, since they are frozen individually, it's a cinch to pop just one or two out of the freezer for a fast lunch or dinner. —POLLY Yield: 6 sandwiches

---

5 tablespoons butter (plus a bit more for buttering the outside of the paninis)

1 tablespoon Worcestershire sauce

½ tablespoon poppy seeds

⅓ cup brown sugar

6 multigrain ciabatta rolls

12 slices all-natural deli ham slices

6 slices Swiss cheese

1. In a medium saucepan, melt the butter over medium-low heat. Add the Worcestershire sauce, poppy seeds, and brown sugar. Stir until combined. Bring the sauce to a boil and cook for 1 minute. Remove from the heat and let the sauce cool for 5 minutes.

2. On a clean surface, slice the rolls horizontally and drizzle about 2 tablespoons of the sauce on the inside of each one. Add 2 slices of ham and a slice of cheese to each. Close the sandwiches up. Butter both the bottom and top of each roll. (*Freezing instructions begin here.*)

3. Cook the paninis using one of the methods below:
METHOD 1: Cook using a panini press or grill press until the bread is crispy on both sides and the cheese is melted. Cooking time will vary depending on the appliance.

METHOD 2: Warm a skillet over medium heat. Place the sandwiches top side down (for easier handling) in the skillet. Use another heavy pan to press the sandwiches down. Cook for 4 to 6 minutes, turning once, until the bread is crispy and the cheese is melted.

Freezer Meal Instructions
TO FREEZE: After Step 2, wrap the uncooked sandwiches individually in foil and freeze in a gallon-size freezer bag.

TO PREPARE FROM FROZEN: Thaw in the refrigerator for 24 hours or use the defrost setting on the microwave, then cook as directed.

SUPER STUFFED BAKED POTATOES

A rich-tasting, twice-stuffed baked potato that you can feel good about? Oh yes. Greek yogurt and chicken broth help replace some of the fat in this typically calorie-laden side dish, while the addition of two superfoods, sweet potato and broccoli, up the nutrition payout. These super spuds are both hearty enough to serve as an entree and decadent enough to serve as a side dish on a special occasion. *Yield: 8 stuffed potatoes (4 servings as a main dish or 8 servings as a side dish)*

4 large russet potatoes

1 large sweet potato

3 cups fresh broccoli florets

¾ cup plain Greek yogurt

1 cup store-bought or homemade Chicken Broth (page 217)

¼ cup softened butter

1½ teaspoons kosher salt

¾ teaspoon ground black pepper

2 tablespoons minced fresh chives

1¼ cups shredded Cheddar cheese, divided

½ pound uncured bacon or turkey bacon, cooked and chopped into bite-size pieces

1. Preheat the oven to 400°F. Wash the potatoes, poke a few holes in each one with a knife, and wrap only the sweet potato in foil (leave the other potatoes unwrapped). Bake on the middle rack for about 1 hour, or until soft in the middle when a knife is inserted. Let them cool enough to handle. Increase the heat to 425°F.

2. While the potatoes bake, fill a medium saucepan about one-third full with water, cover, and bring to a boil. Meanwhile, fill a medium bowl with ice and water. Once the pot of water is boiling, carefully drop the broccoli florets in, cover, and bring back to a boil. Boil for 1 to 2 minutes, or just until fork-tender (undercook just slightly). Remove with a slotted spoon and immediately plunge into the ice water to stop the cooking. Once cooled, lay the broccoli on a towel to dry and then chop into smaller, bite-size pieces that can be stirred into the stuffing mix.

3. Cut all of the potatoes in half. Carefully scoop out the flesh with a spoon and place in a large mixing bowl, making sure to leave a bit of the flesh around all sides to keep the potato skins intact. Discard the sweet potato skin but keep the others. To the mixing bowl, add the yogurt, chicken broth, butter, salt, pepper, and chives. Use a potato masher or the back of a fork to mash and combine the mixture. Using a spoon, gently stir in 1 cup of the cheese, the bacon, and broccoli. Scoop the mixture back into the potato skins evenly. The stuffing will heap over the tops. Sprinkle

(CONTINUED)

GOES WELL WITH

✓ Chili-Rubbed Beef
   Brisket (page 195)

✓ Garden salad

the tops with the remaining $1/4$ cup cheese (about $1^1/_2$ teaspoons per potato half). *(Freezing instructions begin here.)*

4. Place the stuffed potatoes on a foil- or parchment-lined baking sheet and bake for 10 to 15 minutes, or until heated through and golden brown on top.

Freezer Meal Instructions

TO FREEZE: Prepare potatoes through Step 3. Place in a single layer in a 13″ x 9″ freezer container or in 2 gallon-size freezer bags in a single layer. Seal well and freeze.

TO PREPARE FROM FROZEN: Thaw in the refrigerator for 12 to 24 hours or use the defrost setting on the microwave. Bake according to the recipe directions. If the potatoes are still partially frozen, increase the baking time until warmed through. Cover the tops with foil if they begin to brown too much.

Cooking Notes

▶ Many of these cooking steps can be done ahead of time and the ingredients can be refrigerated until it is time to assemble the potatoes.

▶ Another shortcut is to cook the potatoes in the microwave in 2-minute increments until soft.

RED PEPPER, SPINACH, AND FETA CRUSTLESS QUICHE

I adore the bell pepper–spinach veggie combination in all kinds of dishes, but especially in this low-carb, crustless quiche. The feta lends a salty, slightly tangy bite that balances the sweetness of the red pepper perfectly, while the turkey sausage (if you choose to add it) contributes a little kick of heat.

I think it's worth noting that my parents retested this recipe for me a few times, and my dad has told me three separate times how good it is. Believe me, he is *not* a quiche guy. Definitely add this make-ahead meal to your cooking repertoire for a healthy breakfast, lunch box option, or "one-dish wonder" dinner. —RACHEL *Yield: 6–8 servings*

½ pound ground turkey sausage (optional)

1 red bell pepper, seeded and chopped

Pinch of red-pepper flakes

Salt and ground black pepper

2 cloves garlic, minced

5 ounces frozen spinach, thawed and squeezed of all excess moisture

½ cup (4 ounces) crumbled feta cheese

10 large eggs

½ cup milk

½ cup grated Parmesan cheese

¼ cup shredded mozzarella cheese

1. Preheat the oven to 350°F. Coat a 9″ pie pan or an 8″ x 8″ glass or ceramic casserole dish with cooking spray.

2. *(Note: Skip this step if making a vegetarian version.)* In a skillet over medium-high heat, cook the turkey sausage until no longer pink, breaking it up with a wooden spoon as it cooks. Drain. Sprinkle the crumbled meat in the bottom of the pie pan or casserole dish.

3. Wipe the skillet clean with a paper towel, leaving just a little oil behind (or add 1 teaspoon of oil to the pan if making a vegetarian version). Add the bell pepper, red-pepper flakes, and salt and black pepper to taste and cook just until the bell pepper is soft, 4 to 5 minutes. Add the garlic and stir for 30 seconds. Be careful not to burn the garlic. Remove from the heat.

4. Sprinkle the spinach over the turkey sausage. Then spread the bell pepper mixture over the spinach. Top with the feta.

5. In a medium mixing bowl, whisk together the eggs, milk, Parmesan, and ½ teaspoon of ground black pepper. Pour over the top of the casserole. Sprinkle the mozzarella over the top. *(Freezing instructions begin here.)*

(CONTINUED)

6. Bake for 45 to 50 minutes if turkey sausage was included, until the middle is set and the top is golden brown. (Or bake about 35 minutes if sausage was omitted.) Cover with foil during the last 10 to 15 minutes if the top starts to brown too quickly. Let cool slightly. Slice and serve warm. Leftovers can be stored in the fridge and used for breakfast and lunches for up to 5 days.

Freezer Meal Instructions

TO FREEZE: Put the quiche together (through Step 5) but do not bake. Cover tightly with plastic wrap and/or foil. Carefully place in the freezer.

TO PREPARE FROM FROZEN: Thaw for about 24 hours in the refrigerator. Bake according to recipe directions.

Cooking Notes

▶ Place thawed spinach in an older kitchen hand towel and twist it hard to squeeze out excess moisture.

MINI TURKEY AND VEGGIE CHEESEBURGERS

Recipe courtesy of Julie Brasington from Happy Home Fairy

As a full-time working mama, I need quick and easy when it comes to dinner. These turkey cheeseburgers are always the perfect answer, *and* they help me sneak a few extra vegetables into my kids' bellies (knuckle bumps). Our family loves these burgers on whole wheat sandwich thins and served alongside organic frozen French fries and apple slices.

—JULIE BRASINGTON Yield: 8 mini burgers (4 servings)

1¼ pounds ground turkey

1 medium zucchini, trimmed, shredded, and squeezed of excess moisture (about 1 cup)

1 large carrot, shredded (about ½ cup)

2 cloves garlic, minced

2 tablespoons minced fresh parsley or 2 teaspoons dried

1 cup shredded Cheddar cheese

1 teaspoon salt

½ teaspoon ground black pepper

½ teaspoon onion powder

1 tablespoon olive oil

8 mini whole wheat rolls or buns

Lettuce, tomato slices, Cheddar cheese slices, ketchup, mustard (optional)

1. In a large bowl, using clean hands, mix the turkey, zucchini, carrot, garlic, parsley, shredded cheese, salt, pepper, and onion powder.

2. Divide the mixture into 8 equal portions and form into thin patties. *(Freezing instructions begin here.)*

3. In a large skillet, heat the oil over medium heat. Add half of the burgers to the pan, making sure not to overcrowd it. Cook for 8 to 10 minutes, turning once, or until a thermometer inserted in the center of a burger register 165°F and the meat is no longer pink. Repeat with the second batch.

4. Serve on the buns and add your favorite toppings!

Freezer Meal Instructions

TO FREEZE: Form burger patties and place in single layers divided by parchment paper in a gallon-size freezer bag or container and freeze.

TO PREPARE FROM FROZEN: Completely thaw the patties in the refrigerator. Cook according to recipe instructions.

TURKEY PESTO PANINIS

Considering the simplicity of this recipe, I still cannot believe how fabulous these paninis are. While the fresh pesto—oh, do please make your own and freeze it if you can!—brings some great taste to the sandwiches, the sun-dried tomatoes add a punch of flavor that puts them over the top. Wrap these individually in foil and freeze, and then pull out however many you need for quick lunches or dinners. They defrost quickly in the microwave and can be on the table or in your hand in no time when you're on the go. —POLLY Yield: 6 sandwiches

6 whole wheat ciabatta rolls

6 slices (about ½ pound) provolone cheese

½ cup Pesto (page 214)

¼ cup dry-packed sun-dried tomatoes, finely chopped

1 pound all-natural deli turkey slices

2–3 tablespoons softened butter

GOES WELL WITH

✓ Veggie sticks and hummus

✓ Cut-up fruit

1. On a clean surface, slice the ciabatta rolls horizontally. To each roll bottom, add 1 slice of cheese (I like to tear my cheese in half and put a half piece on both the bottom and top), a heaping tablespoon of pesto, ½ tablespoon of sun-dried tomatoes, and a few slices of turkey. Close the sandwiches with the roll tops.

2. Butter the outside of both the bottom and top of the rolls. *(Freezing instructions begin here.)*

3. Cook the paninis using one of the methods below:

METHOD 1: Cook using a panini press or grill press until the bread is crispy on both sides and the cheese is melted. Cooking time will vary depending on the appliance.

METHOD 2: Warm a skillet over medium heat. Place the sandwiches top side down (for easier handling) in the skillet. Use another heavy pan to press the sandwiches down. Cook for 4 to 6 minutes, turning once, or until the bread is crispy and the cheese is melted.

Freezer Meal Instructions

TO FREEZE: Wrap the sandwiches individually in foil, place in a large freezer bag, seal, and freeze.

TO PREPARE FROM FROZEN: Unwrap and thaw using the microwave defrost setting or in the refrigerator for 24 hours. Cook as directed.

Shrimp Coconut Curry
Bowls, *page 141*

seafood

STRAIGHT FROM ALASKA
SALMON BURGERS

For years now, my dad has taken the long journey from Missouri to Alaska to go fishing. He typically comes home with an abundance of halibut, trout, and salmon that he graciously shares with us. While on his trips, my dad has always been skilled at drawing out wisdom from the locals about the best ways to cook and serve the fish he has caught. This recipe was born out of one of his Alaskan conversations, but we've made it even more delicious by tweaking a few ingredients and adding a light bread crumb coating. These burgers retain the salmon flavor and texture but don't have an overpowering fishy taste, making it a great recipe for introducing salmon to kids or the non-fish eater in your life. —POLLY Yield: 6 burgers

1 pound wild salmon fillets, skin removed

2 cups dried whole wheat bread crumbs, divided

2 tablespoons thinly sliced scallions

2 tablespoons minced fresh cilantro

2 teaspoons grated fresh ginger

1 clove garlic, minced

2 large eggs, lightly beaten

2 tablespoons soy sauce

2 tablespoons lemon juice

2 tablespoons olive oil or avocado oil

6 whole wheat buns (optional)

1. Cut the salmon into 1″ chunks and pulse in a food processor 5 or 6 times (do not overprocess). Set aside.

2. In a large mixing bowl, combine 1 cup of the bread crumbs, the scallions, cilantro, ginger, garlic, eggs, soy sauce, and lemon juice. Using your hands, mix in the salmon just until all of the ingredients are combined.

3. Form the mixture into six ½″-thick patties. Spread the remaining 1 cup bread crumbs on a plate and coat both sides of the burgers in them. *(Freezing instructions begin here.)*

4. In a large nonstick skillet, heat the oil over medium heat until it's shimmery and hot. Cook the patties for 4 to 5 minutes on each side, or until golden brown and cooked through. Serve on buns, if desired.

Freezer Meal Instructions

TO FREEZE: Follow the directions through Step 3. Place the uncooked patties in an airtight freezer bag or container in single layers, separated by parchment paper, and freeze.

TO PREPARE FROM FROZEN: Thaw for 24 hours in the refrigerator. Cook according to the recipe instructions.

GOES WELL WITH

✓ Roasted asparagus (recipe available on Thriving Home)

✓ Fresh fruit salad

✓ Asian Slaw (recipe available on Thriving Home)

NOT SO FISHY STICKS

Fish sticks are a childhood staple, no? I grew up on the fried, processed ones from the freezer section and admit I loved them as a kid. So I wondered if a homemade version could ever rival those sticks of yore. Guess what? A minor miracle has occurred in my house: All my kids and even my husband and I like these Not So Fishy Sticks! They are baked and contain only all-natural, wholesome ingredients.

Tilapia is a mild fish that's perfect for the non-fish lover in your home, but cod will work, too. The panko and pecans give the breading some crunch, while the Parmesan and pantry-staple seasonings add great flavor. The best part for busy families is that these healthy fish sticks go from freezer to table in about 15 minutes! —RACHEL

Yield: 6 servings (2–3 sticks per person)

---

1 pound tilapia fillets (thawed, if previously frozen)

¾ teaspoon salt

½ teaspoon ground black pepper

½ cup pecans, pulsed in food processor until consistency of bread crumbs

½ cup finely grated Parmesan cheese

½ cup whole wheat panko bread crumbs (recommended: Kikkoman brand; plain panko bread crumbs will work as a substitution)

1 teaspoon dried parsley, crushed in hand

1 teaspoon garlic powder

1 large egg

Lemon slices, all-natural ketchup, or tartar sauce (optional)

1. Preheat the oven to 475°F. Line a sheet pan with parchment paper or foil, or coat liberally with cooking spray.

2. Pat the fish dry. Cut the fillets into 3" sticks. Season evenly with the salt and pepper on both sides.

3. In a shallow dish or bowl, combine the pecans, cheese, bread crumbs, parsley, and garlic powder. In another bowl, whisk the egg and a splash of water with a fork.

4. To batter each fish stick, dip the fish into the egg mixture and let the excess drip off. Then dip in the bread crumb mixture, coating both sides well. Lay the fish sticks on the sheet pan, making sure they don't touch. Spray the tops of the fish sticks with cooking spray. Turn them over and spray the other side, giving each side a light coating of oil. *(Freezing instructions begin here.)*

5. Bake for 6 to 10 minutes, turning once, or until the fish flakes easily and is no longer translucent in the middle. Serve with a squeeze of fresh lemon and/or ketchup or tartar sauce, if desired.

Freezer Meal Instructions

TO FREEZE: Place the sheet pan with the breaded fish sticks in the freezer for about 2 hours to flash freeze them. Once frozen, place them carefully in a freezer bag or container, squeeze out all the air, seal, and freeze.

GOES WELL WITH

✓ Oven Fries with a Secret Ingredient (recipe available on Thriving Home)

✓ Peas

TO PREPARE FROM FROZEN: Preheat the oven to 475°F. Place the fish sticks on a sheet pan covered in parchment paper, foil, or liberally coated with cooking spray. Bake from frozen for about 15 minutes, or until they flake easily and are no longer translucent inside.

Cooking Notes

▶ You can also crush pecans by hand. Place them in a resealable plastic bag, press out all the air before sealing, and crush with a small pan, flat-bottomed glass, or mallet.

▶ The flash freeze method ensures that the breading will stick when frozen.

▶ For a nut-free option, substitute crushed sunflower seeds for the pecans.

▶ For a gluten-free option, substitute almond meal for the bread crumbs.

ZESTY MARINATED SHRIMP

Citrus and shrimp are a match made in heaven. Combine fresh herbs and ginger with citrus zest and juice, and you have a shrimp dish that makes your tastebuds sing. If you prefer to grill the shrimp, thread them on kebab skewers or use a vegetable or fish rack and simply follow the same cooking times as directed. *Yield: 8 servings*

---

2 pounds frozen large shrimp, peeled and deveined, tails left on

1½ cups olive oil

Zest and juice of 1 large orange

Zest and juice of 1 large lemon

3 tablespoons chopped cilantro

3 tablespoons chopped fresh parsley

2 tablespoons minced or grated fresh ginger

¼ teaspoon crushed red-pepper flakes

¼ teaspoon salt

¼ teaspoon ground black pepper

Lemon wedges, for serving

GOES WELL WITH

✓ Whole wheat couscous or quinoa

✓ Cranberry Spinach Salad with Creamy Citrus Dressing (recipe available on Thriving Home)

1. Thaw the frozen shrimp overnight in the fridge or place in a colander and run under cool water. Set aside in colander to drain.

2. In a large bowl, stir together the oil, orange zest and juice, lemon zest and juice, cilantro, parsley, ginger, red-pepper flakes, salt, and black pepper. *(Freezing instructions begin here.)* Add the shrimp and toss to coat. Cover and refrigerate for 30 minutes, stirring occasionally.

3. Meanwhile, place the top oven rack in the second row from the top, about 3″ from the broiler. Preheat the broiler. Coat a rimmed sheet pan with cooking spray.

4. Remove the shrimp from the marinade and line up on the sheet pan, making sure they don't touch. Broil the shrimp for 2 to 3 minutes. Turn the shrimp over and broil on the second side for 1 to 2 minutes, or until opaque.

5. Transfer to a platter and serve with the lemon wedges.

Freezer Meal Instructions

TO FREEZE: Place the marinade in a freezer bag. Freeze alongside the frozen bag of shrimp.

TO PREPARE FROM FROZEN: Thaw the marinade and shrimp overnight in the refrigerator. Or place the shrimp in a colander and run cool water over them until thawed, and submerge the marinade bag in cool water until thawed. Marinate and cook the shrimp according to the recipe directions.

SHRIMP POT STICKERS WITH SWEET SOY DIPPING SAUCE

eady to challenge yourself a little and cook something different and fun? Both of our families thought this recipe for pot stickers and dipping sauce was a home run. Pot stickers aren't rocket science, but they do take time. If you make the filling and sauce a day ahead, and then concentrate on wrapping and cooking (or freezing) the next day, it's very doable and enjoyable! My 7-year-old daughter even helped me wrap extras to freeze for later, so don't be afraid to recruit help. To save time, buy pre-shredded cabbage and carrots. Our store even has pre-chopped scallions and garlic, too. Look for the wonton wrappers in the refrigerated produce section. —RACHEL Yield: 40 pot stickers (4–6 servings)

---

12 ounces raw small shrimp, peeled and deveined (thawed, if frozen)

1 cup packed shredded cabbage

½ cup packed shredded carrots

½ cup plus 1 tablespoon sliced scallions, divided

1½ teaspoons minced garlic

2 tablespoons minced fresh ginger

2 tablespoons less-sodium soy sauce

1 teaspoon sesame oil

1 teaspoon Sriracha hot chili sauce, or to taste (optional)

Cornstarch

48 wonton wrappers

8 tablespoons peanut oil

Sweet Soy Dipping Sauce (recipe on page 140)

1. Preheat the oven to 200°F. In a food processor, combine the shrimp, cabbage, carrots, ½ cup of the scallions, the garlic, ginger, soy sauce, sesame oil, and hot sauce. Pulse about 10 times. Scrape down the sides with a spatula and pulse a few more times until the mixture is combined and the vegetables are chopped, but don't pulse so much that it forms a paste. You still want to see the vegetable pieces.

2. Dust a large piece of parchment paper or a clean counter surface with cornstarch (to prevent sticking) and lay out 12 of the wonton wrappers. Place a rounded teaspoon of the filling in the middle of each one. Use your finger to brush a little water along the sides of half of the wonton. Fold the wrapper in half to form a triangle and seal by pinching the edges together. Work quickly and cover the wontons with a moist towel to prevent drying, as needed. If you want to wait a few hours before cooking, place the pot stickers on a plate dusted with cornstarch, cover with plastic wrap, and refrigerate. *(Freezing instructions begin here.)*

3. In a large nonstick skillet, heat 2 tablespoons of the oil over medium-high heat. Add 12 dumplings, one at a time; they can touch one another, but should still be flat in 1 layer. Cook for about 2 minutes, or until the bottoms are lightly browned and most of the oil has been absorbed. Carefully turn them over with a spatula or fork. Add ¼ cup water and cover with a lid. Reduce the heat to

(CONTINUED)

medium and simmer for about 3 minutes. Uncover, increase the heat to medium high, and cook another minute or two, until the bottoms are brown and crisp and the water evaporates.

4. Transfer the pot stickers to a baking sheet and keep warm in the oven. Repeat with the remaining oil and pot stickers. Serve warm with the Sweet Soy Dipping Sauce and garnished with the remaining 1 tablespoon scallions.

SWEET SOY DIPPING SAUCE

3 tablespoons less-sodium soy sauce

3 tablespoons honey

1 tablespoon rice vinegar or white vinegar

1 teaspoon sesame oil

1 tablespoon sliced scallions

Sriracha or hot sauce, to taste

In a small saucepan, combine the soy sauce, honey, vinegar, sesame oil, scallions, and hot sauce and bring to a boil. Reduce the heat and simmer for 3 minutes. Serve alongside the pot stickers in small bowls for dipping.

Freezer Meal Instructions

TO FREEZE: Sprinkle the uncooked pot stickers with cornstarch; freeze on a baking sheet until firm, 1 to 2 hours. Place in a freezer bag and freeze for up to 2 months. Make the Sweet Soy Dipping Sauce and let cool completely. Pour into a freezer container or bag and freeze with the pot stickers.

TO PREPARE FROM FROZEN: Cook from frozen, according to the instructions in Step 3, but simmer for 4 to 5 minutes (instead of 3 minutes, as listed in the recipe). Run the frozen dipping sauce container or bag under warm water just until it is thawed enough to dump into a pot. Warm over medium-low heat, stirring occasionally, until completely thawed and warmed through.

GOES WELL WITH

✓ Brown rice

✓ Asian Slaw (recipe available on Thriving Home)

✓ Orange slices

SHRIMP COCONUT CURRY BOWLS

Mmmm-mmm! When I want to surprise my husband with a date night dinner, this is my go-to one-dish wonder. Although there is a little kick to the sauce, my 7-year-old daughter even laps these noodles up and then requests them in her lunch the next day. But feel free to cut back on the Sriracha or kick it up to your liking. Do not skip the fresh toppings at the end, though. The shredded cabbage, chopped peanuts, and squeeze of lime make these curry bowls to die for! —RACHEL *Yield: 4 servings*

COCONUT CURRY SAUCE

1 tablespoon olive oil or avocado oil

½ yellow onion, diced

1 tablespoon minced fresh ginger

2 tablespoons red curry paste

1 can (14 ounces) unsweetened coconut milk

1½ tablespoons sugar

1 teaspoon Sriracha hot chili sauce, plus more to taste

1 tablespoon fish sauce

2 tablespoons soy sauce

⅓ cup store-bought or homemade Chicken Broth (page 217, optional, if you like it soupier)

SHRIMP BOWLS

4 ounces soba noodles or whole wheat angel hair pasta

2 tablespoons olive or avocado oil, divided

1 pound peeled and deveined raw shrimp

Salt and ground black pepper

1 bag (16 ounces) frozen stir-fry vegetables or 3 cups fresh chopped vegetables like carrots, broccoli, and green beans

1 cup shredded purple cabbage, for serving

Chopped peanuts, for serving

4 lime wedges, for serving

---

1. *To make the sauce:* In a 2-quart saucepan, heat the oil over medium heat. Add the onion and ginger and sauté for 3 to 4 minutes, or until soft. Add the curry paste and cook for 1 minute. Stir in the coconut milk, sugar, hot sauce, fish sauce, soy sauce, and broth (if desired). Simmer for 15 to 20 minutes, or until reduced and thickened a bit, although it will still be a soupy consistency at the end. Stir occasionally. Taste and add more hot sauce, if desired. (*Freezing instructions begin here.*)

2. *To make the bowls:* Prepare the noodles according to package directions and drain. Set aside and toss with a little oil to keep from sticking.

3. Meanwhile, in a large skillet, heat 1 tablespoon of the oil over medium-high heat. Pat the shrimp dry and season lightly with salt and pepper. Stir-fry the shrimp for 2 to 3 minutes, or until opaque. Set aside.

4. Add the remaining 1 tablespoon oil to the pan. Add the frozen vegetables and stir-fry for 5 to 7 minutes, or until tender-crisp. Remove the pan from the heat.

(CONTINUED)

GOES WELL WITH

✓ Shrimp Pot
Stickers with Sweet
Soy Dipping Sauce
(page 138)

5. *To assemble:* Add the noodles, shrimp, and sauce to the veggies and gently toss together until combined. Divide among 4 bowls. Serve each bowl topped with the cabbage, peanuts, and a lime wedge.

Freezer Meal Instructions

TO FREEZE: After preparing the sauce in Step 1, freeze in a freezer container or bag next to the frozen shrimp and frozen vegetables.

TO PREPARE FROM FROZEN: You will need to have pasta, purple cabbage, peanuts, and lime wedges on hand. Thaw the shrimp in the refrigerator or in a colander by running cool water over them. Thaw the sauce in the refrigerator or using the defrost setting of the microwave. (*Note:* Do not thaw the frozen vegetables.) Follow the cooking instructions starting with Step 2.

Cooking Notes

▶ There really is no substitution for fresh ginger in this recipe. I've tried dried ginger, and it simply doesn't work. Make sure you have fresh ginger on hand and wrap and freeze the extra for another time.

MINI CRAB CAKES WITH CREAMY HERB DIPPING SAUCE

Years ago, I took a group of high school girls, who happened to be foodies, to Charleston over spring break. I fell in love with the city and with crab cakes on that trip. Despite living 1,000 miles away from the ocean, I was determined to make my own version at home. Thankfully, you can find lump crabmeat at almost any grocery store now, and even canned crab meat will work in a pinch or as a cheaper option. But imitation crab meat will *not* work. These Mini Crab Cakes are such a treat for our family, especially when served alongside the creamy, lemony dipping sauce. —RACHEL Yield: 12 mini crab cakes (4–6 servings)

---

1 large egg, beaten

2 tablespoons minced scallions, green parts only

2 tablespoons finely chopped fresh parsley

¼ cup real mayonnaise

Juice of half a lemon (about 2 teaspoons)

1 tablespoon Dijon mustard

2 teaspoons Old Bay seasoning

¼ teaspoon ground black pepper

¾ cup whole wheat panko bread crumbs, divided

1 pound lump crabmeat, picked over for shells

½ cup olive oil or avocado oil, divided

Lemon wedges, for serving

Creamy Herb Dipping Sauce, for serving (recipe on page 146)

1. Line a baking sheet with foil.

2. In a mixing bowl, combine the egg, scallions, parsley, mayonnaise, lemon juice, mustard, Old Bay, pepper, and ¼ cup of the bread crumbs. Gently stir in the crab meat until combined.

3. Scoop ¼ cup of the crab mixture per patty and form into twelve 2½" x ½" patties. *(Freezing instructions begin here.)* Place on the lined pan, cover with plastic wrap, and refrigerate for at least 30 minutes and up to 24 hours. This will help the cakes stay together better.

4. Spread the remaining ½ cup bread crumbs on a plate. Gently press the crab cakes into the bread crumbs on one side and use your fingers to spread bread crumbs over the top side.

5. In a large pan, heat ¼ cup of the oil over medium heat until hot and shimmery. Place half of the crab cakes in the pan, making sure they do not touch. Be careful, as oil may splatter. Cook for 4 to 6 minutes, turning once, or until golden brown on each side. Transfer the cakes to a serving platter, wipe the pan clean with a paper towel, and add the remaining ¼ cup oil to the pan. When the oil is hot, add the second batch of crab cakes and cook as directed above.

6. Serve with lemon wedges and Creamy Herb Dipping Sauce (or your favorite seafood sauce).

(CONTINUED)

Yield: generous
½ cup (enough for
4–6 servings of
crab cakes)

½ cup real mayonnaise

2½ tablespoons fresh
lemon juice

2 tablespoons minced
fresh parsley leaves

1 teaspoon minced
fresh thyme leaves or
¼ teaspoon dried
thyme

1 tablespoon minced
scallion, white and
green parts

½ teaspoon salt

¼ teaspoon ground
black pepper

GOES WELL WITH

✓ Boiled Baby
Potatoes (recipe
available on
Thriving Home)

✓ Corn on the cob

✓ Coleslaw

CREAMY HERB DIPPING SAUCE

In a small bowl, combine the mayonnaise, lemon juice, parsley, thyme, scallion, salt, and pepper. Cover and refrigerate for at least 30 minutes. The sauce can be refrigerated for up to 5 days, but it does not freeze.

Freezer Meal Instructions

TO FREEZE: After forming the patties in Step 3, do not refrigerate. Spread ½ cup bread crumbs on a plate. Gently press the crab cakes into the bread crumbs on one side and use your fingers to spread bread crumbs over the top side. Place the crab cakes in a gallon-size freezer bag or container in single layers, using parchment paper between layers so they don't stick together. Freeze. *(Note: Dipping sauce cannot be frozen. It must be made fresh.)*

TO PREPARE FROM FROZEN: Let the crab cakes thaw in the refrigerator overnight and keep cold until ready to cook. Make the Creamy Herb Dipping Sauce and refrigerate at least 30 minutes before serving. Panfry the cakes according to the recipe directions starting with Step 5. Serve warm with lemon wedges and dipping sauce (or your favorite seafood sauce).

Cooking Notes

▶ Crab cakes are very fragile. Although refrigerating them beforehand will help them stay together, handle them carefully throughout the cooking process.

PESTO AND FETA TUNA MELTS

Canned tuna can get a bad rap sometimes, but think about all the advantages: It's cheap, shelf stable, and full of omega-3s and lean protein, and kids often love it. Even if you didn't grow up on tuna salad or tuna casserole, I think you'll enjoy this easy, modern twist on a tuna melt. My inspiration was the Tuna, Pesto, and Feta Sandwich I always order at Murry's, a favorite restaurant of mine in town. This open-faced whole grain version makes for a seriously tasty and nutritious lunch or dinner. If you want to add in some vegetables, add a tomato slice or baby spinach leaves under the cheese slice right before broiling. —RACHEL Yield: 6 tuna melts

---

1 whole grain baguette (or 3 whole grain ciabatta rolls or English muffins)

2 cans (5 ounces each) tuna, drained

4 ounces crumbled feta cheese

1 tablespoon Dijon mustard

1 tablespoon fresh lemon juice (about half a lemon)

¼ teaspoon ground black pepper (or more to taste)

2 tablespoons olive oil

1½ tablespoons minced fresh chives

6 tablespoons Pesto (page 214)

6 slices provolone cheese

1. Preheat the broiler. Line a sheet pan with foil or parchment paper for easy cleanup.

2. Slice the baguette in half lengthwise and then cut each half into 3 equal pieces, so you'll end up with 6 pieces total. (Or split the rolls or muffins.)

3. In a bowl, use a fork to combine the tuna, feta cheese, mustard, lemon juice, pepper, olive oil, and chives.

4. Spread 1 tablespoon of the pesto on each piece of bread. Evenly divide the tuna mixture among the bread pieces and spread out using the back of a spoon. Top each piece with a slice of provolone cheese. *(Freezing instructions begin here.)*

5. Broil the open-faced sandwiches for 2 to 2½ minutes, or until the cheese is melted and golden on top. Serve warm.

Freezer Meal Instructions

TO FREEZE: Make the sandwiches through Step 4. Wrap each in foil or plastic wrap and freeze in a gallon-size freezer bag or container.

TO PREPARE FROM FROZEN: Thaw overnight in the refrigerator and then set out on the counter to bring up to room temperature (30 minutes at the most). Broil according to the recipe directions. If the tuna mixture is still cold after broiling, microwave in 10-second increments.

Cooking Notes
▶ This recipe also works well in a toaster oven.

English Muffin Pizzas, *page 160*

pasta, pizza, and more

BAKED CHICKEN AND BROCCOLI ALFREDO

We've taken a classic comfort dish and turned it into a freezer-friendly, easy-to-make dinner. While I personally like the broccoli roughly chopped, the more finely chopped it is, the more it disappears into the sauce. It can be a great way to sneak in some greens for picky eaters! You didn't hear me say this, but ... to make this dish extra decadent, add 1 cup of cooked and chopped bacon to the Alfredo sauce. This is a hearty, crowd-pleasing dish that will provide you with some great leftovers for days. —POLLY Yield: 6 (hearty) servings

---

12 ounces whole wheat penne pasta

1½ tablespoons olive oil or avocado oil

6 cloves garlic, minced

4½ tablespoons unbleached all-purpose flour

1½ cups store-bought or homemade Chicken Broth (page 217)

1½ cups whole milk

1½ cups freshly grated Parmesan cheese

1 teaspoon salt

½ teaspoon ground black pepper

2 cups chopped cooked chicken (about 2 small chicken breasts)

2 cups chopped broccoli

1½ cups shredded mozzarella cheese

GOES WELL WITH

✓ Garlic Bread (recipe available on Thriving Home)

1. Preheat the oven to 375°F. Coat a 13" x 9" casserole dish with cooking spray.

2. In a large stockpot with well-salted water, cook the pasta until al dente according to package directions.

3. Meanwhile, prepare the Alfredo sauce. In a large skillet, heat the oil over medium-high heat. Add the garlic and cook, stirring, for 1 minute. Sprinkle with the flour and stir continuously for 1 minute, being careful not to burn it. Slowly pour in the chicken broth, whisking to combine until smooth. Whisk in the milk and bring the mixture to a simmer. Cook for an additional 1 to 2 minutes, or until thickened. Stir in the Parmesan, salt, and pepper until the cheese is melted. Remove from the heat and set aside.

4. Drain the cooked pasta. Add the chicken, broccoli, and Alfredo sauce. Gently toss to combine until the pasta is evenly coated.

5. Pour the pasta into the casserole dish and top with the mozzarella. *(Freezing instructions begin here.)* Bake for 20 to 25 minutes, or until the cheese is melted and just starts to brown. Serve immediately.

Freezer Meal Instructions

TO FREEZE: Put the casserole together completely, but do not bake. Wrap tightly in a few layers of plastic wrap and foil (or a lid), squeezing out all excess air, and freeze.

TO PREPARE FROM FROZEN: Let thaw for 24 hours in the refrigerator and bake as directed.

CREAMY CITRUS PASTA WITH SHRIMP

I t's not very often that a creamy pasta can taste so fresh and light. Thanks to the citrus zest and chopped basil, this out-of-the-ordinary casserole is incredibly flavorful. The addition of shrimp to the recipe adds a lean protein and some texture while not weighing it down. For a bit more color, sprinkle chopped parsley over the top after baking. Add some chopped fresh mint leaves into the cream along with the basil to add additional fresh flavor. Yield: 8 servings

1 tablespoon olive oil or avocado oil

1 pound raw shrimp, peeled and deveined

1¼ teaspoons salt, divided

¼ teaspoon ground black pepper

12 ounces whole wheat angel hair pasta

2 cups heavy cream

¼ cup dry sherry

Zest of 2 lemons

Zest of 2 oranges

24 leaves fresh basil, chopped or torn

1 cup grated Parmesan cheese

½ cup shredded mozzarella cheese

GOES WELL WITH

✓ Cranberry Spinach Salad with Citrus Dressing (recipe available on Thriving Home)

✓ Orange slices

1. Preheat the oven to 375°F. Coat a 13″ x 9″ baking dish with cooking spray.

2. In a large skillet, heat the oil over medium heat. Season the shrimp with ¼ teaspoon of the salt and the pepper. Cook for 2 to 3 minutes, or until opaque. Transfer to a plate, allow to cool slightly, and chop into small pieces. Set aside.

3. Bring a large pot of well-salted water to a boil and add the pasta. Cook until al dente, according to package directions. Drain and pour back into the pot.

4. While the pasta is cooking, in a medium saucepan, warm the cream over medium-low heat. Add the sherry, lemon and orange zest, and the remaining 1 teaspoon salt; simmer for 7 to 10 minutes. Remove from the heat and stir in the basil.

5. Pour the cream mixture over the pasta and toss until well coated. Slowly sprinkle in the Parmesan and stir until combined. Stir in the shrimp. Pour the pasta mixture into the baking dish and top with the mozzarella. *(Freezing instructions begin here.)*

6. Bake for about 10 minutes (or longer, if baking from cold), or until the cheese has melted and the top begins to brown slightly.

Freezer Meal Instructions

TO FREEZE: Prepare the casserole, but do not bake. Wrap the dish tightly in several layers of plastic wrap and 1 or 2 layers of foil, squeeze out excess air, and freeze.

TO PREPARE FROM FROZEN: Let the dish thaw in the refrigerator for 24 hours. Set out on the counter for about 30 minutes to bring to room temperature, and then bake as directed.

BAKED PINK PASTA WITH SAUSAGE

You know a recipe is a win when, mid-dinner, family members are already asking about the next time we will have it. This was the case with this baked pasta. This has also become one of my favorite recipes to make for large groups, because it's liked by all ages and easy to make ahead and either freeze or refrigerate until it's time to bake it. Serve with some garlic bread and a simple salad, and you will have a home run meal to make again and again. —POLLY

Yield: 8 servings

2 pounds whole wheat penne pasta

2 tablespoons olive oil or avocado oil

½ cup chopped onion

¾ cup diced green bell pepper (about 1 bell pepper)

6 cloves garlic, minced

1½ pounds ground Italian sausage

1 cup water

1 jar (28 ounces) all-natural Alfredo sauce or Easy Alfredo Sauce (recipe follows)

1 can (18 ounces) tomato sauce

2 cups shredded mozzarella cheese, plus additional for top, if desired

1. Preheat the oven to 350°F. Coat a 13″ x 9″ baking dish with cooking spray.

2. In a large stockpot, cook the pasta until al dente according to package directions. Drain and return to the pot.

3. Meanwhile, in a large skillet, heat the oil over medium-high heat. Add the onion and bell pepper. Cook, stirring frequently, until they begin to soften, 4 to 5 minutes. Add the garlic and cook for 1 minute.

4. Add the sausage and water. Use a potato masher or fork to work all the lumps out of the sausage. Cook, stirring frequently, until the sausage is no longer pink, about 5 minutes.

5. Add the sausage mixture, Alfredo sauce, tomato sauce, and mozzarella to the pasta. Stir to combine.

6. Transfer to the baking dish and sprinkle with additional cheese on top, if desired. *(Freezing instructions begin here.)*

7. Bake for 30 minutes, or until golden brown and bubbly.

(CONTINUED)

EASY ALFREDO SAUCE

1 pint heavy cream

½ cup butter

1½ cups grated Parmesan cheese

In a medium saucepan over medium-low heat, combine the cream, butter, and cheese. Stir and cook until warmed through, about 5 minutes. Remove from the heat. Sauce will thicken upon standing.

Freezer Meal Instructions

TO FREEZE: Assemble the casserole completely, but do not bake. Wrap the dish tightly in several layers of plastic wrap and 1 or 2 layers of foil, squeeze out excess air, and freeze.

TO PREPARE FROM FROZEN: Thaw in the refrigerator for 24 hours. Set out on the counter for about 30 minutes to bring to room temperature, and then bake as directed.

GOES WELL WITH

✓ Chopped salad

✓ Pears

CREAMY TOMATO PENNE WITH SHRIMP

Here's yet another recipe that my Freezer Club from back in the day requested over and over. Be sure to pat yourself on the back after making this elegant dish, because it is a treat. Serve with your favorite crisp white wine and side salad for a romantic meal with that special person in your life. —RACHEL Yield: 6 servings

12 ounces whole wheat penne pasta

1½ tablespoons unsalted butter, divided

1½ tablespoons olive oil, divided

1 pound peeled and deveined raw shrimp

Salt and ground black pepper

1 small onion, finely diced

2 cloves garlic, minced

¼ teaspoon red-pepper flakes

½ cup dry white wine or chicken broth

1 can (15 ounces) tomato sauce

1 cup half-and-half

¼ cup loosely packed chopped fresh parsley

3 leaves fresh basil, chopped into long, thin strips (chiffonade)

Freshly grated Parmesan cheese, for serving

1. *(If freezing, skip Step 1 and begin with Step 2.)* Cook the pasta according to package directions until al dente. Drain and return to the pot. Toss with a little olive oil to keep from sticking.

2. Meanwhile, in a large skillet, heat ½ tablespoon each of the butter and olive oil over medium-high heat. Add the shrimp and season lightly with a pinch of salt and black pepper. Cook and stir for 2 minutes, or until opaque. Do not overcook. Set aside on a plate.

3. Wipe out the skillet, and melt the remaining 1 tablespoon each butter and olive oil. Add the onion, garlic, and red-pepper flakes and cook, stirring frequently, for about 3 minutes, or until translucent. Season lightly with salt and pepper as the mixture cooks.

4. Pour in the wine or broth and simmer for 1 minute. Stir in the tomato sauce. Reduce the heat to low and stir in the half-and-half.

5. *Optional, if you like a smooth sauce:* Using a ladle, carefully pour the sauce into a blender and blend until smooth. Return to the pan.

6. Chop the shrimp into bite-size pieces and stir into the sauce. Taste and season with salt and pepper to taste. Toss in the parsley and basil and stir to combine. *(Freezing instructions begin here.)*

7. Pour the sauce over the pasta and stir gently to combine. Serve warm with freshly grated Parmesan cheese on top.

GOES WELL WITH

✓ Crusty bakery
  bread

✓ Side salad

Freezer Meal Instructions

TO FREEZE: Do not cook the pasta. Follow Steps 2 through 6. Let sauce cool completely and freeze in a freezer container or bag. Squeeze out air and seal well.

TO PREPARE FROM FROZEN: Let the sauce thaw completely in the refrigerator for about 24 hours. Heat gently over low heat just until warm, stirring occasionally. Or warm in the microwave in 45-second increments, stirring each time, just until warmed through. Cook the penne pasta according to package directions and serve with the pasta sauce and Parmesan cheese on top.

Cooking Notes

▶ When reheating this dish, just heat until warmed through so the shrimp doesn't get tough.

CHICKEN PESTO PIZZA

No need to go to a restaurant for gourmet pizza. You can make it right at home tonight! On top of a homemade crust, the fresh flavor of pesto is complemented by chicken and red bell peppers. All of this goodness is topped off with melty cheese and a zing from chopped scallions. A shout-out to our friend Nicole for providing the inspiration for this recipe.

Yield: one 16" pizza

2 teaspoons olive oil or avocado oil

1 large (about ¾ pound) chicken breast, cut into ½" pieces

1 teaspoon garlic salt

¼ teaspoon ground black pepper

1 red bell pepper, seeded and cut into thin strips

1 teaspoon dried oregano

Whole Wheat Pizza Dough (page 215), rolled out into a 16" circle or a purchased pizza crust

½ cup Pesto (page 214)

½ teaspoon red-pepper flakes

2 cups shredded mozzarella cheese, divided

½ cup feta cheese

2 tablespoons chopped scallions

½ cup shredded Parmesan cheese

1. Preheat the oven to 450°F (or, if using a purchased pizza crust, whatever the directions call for on the package). Line a baking sheet with parchment paper.

2. In a large skillet, heat the oil over medium heat. Season the chicken with the garlic salt and black pepper. Place the chicken and bell pepper in the skillet. Season with the oregano and a bit more salt and black pepper, to taste. Cook, stirring occasionally, until the chicken is no longer pink, 4 to 5 minutes. Set aside.

3. Place the pizza dough or crust on the baking sheet. Spread the pesto over the pizza dough. Sprinkle the red-pepper flakes, 1 cup of the mozzarella, and the feta evenly over the pesto. Arrange the chicken mixture on top. Top with the remaining 1 cup mozzarella, the scallions, and Parmesan. *(Freezing instructions begin here.)*

4. Bake for 15 to 18 minutes, or until golden brown on top.

Freezer Meal Instructions

TO FREEZE: Assemble the pizza on top of a baking sheet lined with parchment paper. Instead of baking it, stick it in the freezer until fully frozen through, about 2 hours. Wrap frozen pizza tightly in several layers of plastic wrap and then 1 or 2 layers of foil and freeze.

TO PREPARE FROM FROZEN: Let the pizza thaw in the refrigerator for 24 hours. Bake as instructed.

GOES WELL WITH

✓ Salad with Balsamic Dressing with Herbs (recipe available on Thriving Home)

ENGLISH MUFFIN PIZZAS

This recipe probably wins the award for being the easiest meal in the book. We especially love it because it is one of those meals that can be baked straight from frozen and is a great way to use up leftover ingredients. Be sure to involve the kids in this one; it's pretty hard to mess up, and they'll love the process of customizing their own pizza. Yield: 12 mini pizzas

6 whole wheat English muffins

¾ cup Pizza Sauce (page 213)

2¼ cups shredded mozzarella cheese

1 cup finely chopped toppings: pepperoni, cooked Italian sausage, green peppers, banana peppers, spinach, mushrooms, etc.

GOES WELL WITH

✓ Grapes

✓ Garden salad

1. Preheat the broiler. Line a baking sheet with parchment paper or foil.

2. Cut each English muffin horizontally and lay them out on the baking sheet with the inside facing up. Broil for 2 to 3 minutes, or just until they start to brown. Remove from the oven.

3. Reduce the heat to 375°F.

4. Add about 1 tablespoon of pizza sauce to each muffin half. Sprinkle about 2 tablespoons of cheese over the sauce.

5. Mix together the chopped topping ingredients of your choice and scoop a heaping tablespoon of the mix on top of the cheese.

6. Top each off with another tablespoon of cheese. (*Freezing instructions begin here.*)

7. Bake for about 10 minutes, or until the cheese has thoroughly melted.

Freezer Meal Instructions

TO FREEZE: Prepare as directed, but do not bake. Flash freeze on the baking sheet until completely frozen, 1 to 2 hours. Place in an airtight freezer container or bag, separating layers with parchment paper.

TO PREPARE FROM FROZEN: In a preheated 375°F oven, bake from frozen for 13 to 15 minutes.

Cooking Notes

▶ Chopping up the toppings into small pieces makes it easier to spread them out over such a small space.

CHEESY LASAGNA POCKETS

What are Lasagna Pockets, you ask? Well, imagine if a pizza pocket and a lasagna made a baby. This is one of the most requested meals by my kids. I literally have to put a cap on how many they can eat at dinner. These also make for a delicious lunch the next day. I even send them warm and wrapped in foil in my children's lunch boxes, along with some dipping sauce.

This recipe is fairly time intensive if you make the dough and sauce from scratch, so it may not be a good pick for a Freezer Party or Freezer Club. But you'll want to double the recipe and save all of these for yourself anyway! It's so easy to pull a pocket out of the freezer, warm it up, and go. One shortcut you can take it is to buy a large premade pizza dough ball at your favorite pizzeria in place of the homemade dough. You can also use your favorite all-natural, organic pizza sauce to save time. —RACHEL Yield: 8 pockets

---

1 container (15 ounces) ricotta cheese

½ cup grated Parmesan cheese

1½ cups grated mozzarella cheese

3 large eggs, divided

¼ cup minced fresh parsley

½ teaspoon dried oregano, crushed in hand

½ teaspoon salt

¼ teaspoon ground black pepper

¼ teaspoon garlic powder

Whole Wheat Pizza Dough (page 215)

Pizza Sauce (page 213), for dipping

1. Adjust the oven racks so both are equidistant from the top and bottom. Preheat the oven to 425°F. Line 2 sheet pans with foil or parchment paper.

2. In a medium bowl, stir together the ricotta, Parmesan, mozzarella, 2 of the eggs, the parsley, oregano, salt, pepper, and garlic powder. Set aside.

3. On a well-floured surface, roll the dough into a round disk shape. Divide it into 8 equal parts, cutting it like a pizza. Use your hands to shape each section into a ball. Then, using a floured rolling pin, roll each ball out into a very thin circle (less than ⅛" thick).

4. Spoon about 2 tablespoons of filling onto half of each dough circle, leaving a little room around the edges. (Do not overfill or the pocket will split open while baking.) Fold the dough in half over the filling and press the edges tightly to seal. Use the back of a fork to make sure it's sealed well. Then use the fork to poke a few holes in the top of each pocket. Carefully transfer to the sheet pans, making sure to leave a little room between the pockets.

5. In a small bowl, beat the remaining egg and a splash of water. Brush the surface of each pocket with the egg wash.

(CONTINUED)

6. Place both sheet pans in the oven and bake for 16 to 18 minutes, or until golden brown on top. Be sure to switch the pans from top to bottom and turn from front to back halfway through the baking time to ensure even baking. *(Freezing instructions begin here.)* Serve with warm pizza sauce for dipping.

Freezer Meal Instructions

TO FREEZE: Bake according to recipe instructions. Let pockets cool completely. Place in an airtight freezer bag or container in single layers, using parchment paper between layers. Freeze.

TO PREPARE FROM FROZEN: Wrap a frozen pocket in a moist paper towel. Microwave on the defrost setting until warmed through. Serve with warm pizza sauce for dipping.

Cooking Notes

▶ If you want to add meat, just spoon about 1 to 2 teaspoons of crumbled, browned Italian sausage or chopped uncured pepperoni on top of the filling in each pocket before closing.

▶ To include more vegetables, add 1 to 2 teaspoons of chopped baby spinach or chopped, sautéed bell peppers on top of the filling in each pocket before closing.

MAKE-YOUR-OWN CALZONES

A handheld, folded-up pizza? Whoever created the calzone was a genius! I always double this recipe because, like the Cheesy Lasagna Pockets, they are perfect for those weeknights, filled with soccer practice or music lessons, when you have to eat in shifts. Invite your family members to stuff their individual calzones with their favorite toppings. Then fold, seal, and use a fork to poke holes in the top, spelling the first letter of their name. Or you can create batches such as "pepperoni," "veggie," or "plain cheese" to have on hand. I just pull however many I need from the freezer and warm them quickly in the microwave. —RACHEL

Yield: 8 calzones

Whole Wheat Pizza Dough (page 215)

2 cups shredded mozzarella cheese

1 cup Pizza Sauce, plus 3 cups for dipping (page 213)

½ cup finely shredded Parmesan cheese

½–¾ cup additional toppings of choice: additional shredded cheese of your choice (provolone, Asiago, Parmesan, etc.); chopped baby spinach; cooked and crumbled all-natural ground sausage; chopped uncured turkey pepperoni; chopped and sautéed bell peppers, onions, or mushrooms; sliced black olives)

1 large egg, beaten

1. Adjust the oven racks so both are equidistant from the top and bottom. Preheat the oven to 425°F. Line 2 sheet pans with parchment paper or foil.

2. On a well-floured surface, roll the dough into a round disk shape. Divide it into 8 equal parts, cutting it like a pizza. Use your hands to shape each section into a ball. Then, using a floured rolling pin, roll the ball out into a very thin circle (less than $^1/_8''$ thick).

3. On half of each rolled-out calzone, place $^1/_4$ cup mozzarella, 2 tablespoons pizza sauce, 1 tablespoon Parmesan, and 1 rounded tablespoon of your favorite topping. (Do not overfill.)

4. Fold each calzone in half so that the edges meet. Seal by folding the edges over each other and pressing down with a fork. With the fork, poke a few holes in the tops. Carefully transfer to the sheet pans, making sure to leave a little room between them.

5. In a small bowl, whisk the egg and a splash of water. Using a pastry brush or paper towel, spread the egg wash over the tops of the calzones.

6. Place both sheet pans in the oven and bake for 16 to 18 minutes, or until golden brown on top. *Note*: Be sure to switch the pans from top to bottom and turn from front to back halfway through the baking time to ensure even baking. (*Freezing instructions begin here.*)

7. Let cool slightly on the sheet pans and serve with warm pizza sauce for dipping.

✓ Side salad

✓ Cut-up fruit

Freezer Meal Instructions

TO FREEZE: Bake the calzones and cool completely. Place in a gallon-size freezer bag, pressing out all the air before sealing.

TO PREPARE FROM FROZEN: Wrap frozen calzones individually in a moist paper towel and microwave in 30-second increments until warmed through. Serve calzones with warm pizza sauce for dipping.

Cooking Notes

▸ One shortcut you can take is to buy a large premade pizza dough ball at your favorite pizzeria. You can also use your favorite all-natural, organic pizza sauce to save time.

PESTO CHICKEN LASAGNA ROLLS

"Mom, these are way yum!" My 5-year-old articulated what we were all thinking about these rolls after we tried them for the first time. Big flavor. Crowd pleaser. Way yum. I think using fresh pesto in this recipe makes all the difference, so take the extra step to make your own if you can. As an added bonus, serving lasagna in the roll-up form makes this dish versatile when it comes to freezing as you can freeze portions individually or as one big dish.

—POLLY Yield: 18 rolls (about 8 servings)

2½ cups diced cooked chicken breasts

1 cup shredded Parmesan cheese

3 cups shredded mozzarella cheese, divided

1 container (15 ounces) ricotta cheese

1 cup Pesto (page 214)

3 cups Slow Cooker Marinara Sauce (page 212), divided

18 whole wheat lasagna noodles, cooked and tossed with a little olive oil to prevent sticking

GOES WELL WITH
✓ Steamed broccoli
✓ Fruit salad

1. Preheat the oven to 350°F. Coat a 13″ x 9″ baking dish with cooking spray.

2. In a medium mixing bowl, stir together the chicken, Parmesan, 1 cup of the mozzarella, the ricotta, and pesto.

3. Spread about 1 cup of the marinara sauce evenly over the bottom of the baking dish.

4. On a baking sheet, lay out the cooked lasagna noodles and spread about ⅔ cup of the chicken mixture evenly over each noodle. Roll each up and place seam side down in the dish. Repeat, placing rolls closely together.

5. Scoop a heaping spoonful of marinara sauce over each roll and then top with the remaining 2 cups mozzarella. *(Freezing instructions begin here.)*

6. Bake for 20 minutes, or until warmed through and bubbly.

Freezer Meal Instructions

TO FREEZE: Assemble the lasagna rolls completely, but do not bake. Wrap the dish tightly in several layers of plastic wrap and 1 or 2 layers of foil, squeeze out excess air, and freeze.

TO PREPARE FROM FROZEN: Thaw in the refrigerator for 24 hours. Set out on the counter for about 30 minutes to bring to room temperature, and then bake as directed.

MEAT LOVER'S LASAGNA

As you've probably gathered by the name, this lasagna is not for the faint of heart. It is packed with rich flavor, bold seasonings, and, you guessed it, *meat*. Years ago, I snagged the recipe from my friend Jen, who inherited it from her grandma. I speculate that it's been passed down over the generations because dudes-husbands-sons-guys-dads-nephews love it. Our whole food tweaks have not compromised the flavor or heartiness one bit. It's a guaranteed win for your big eater(s). Yield: 9 servings

---

2 tablespoons olive oil or avocado oil

½ large yellow onion, diced

3 cloves garlic, minced

1 pound lean ground beef

1 pound ground Italian sausage (we use mild)

2 cans (15 ounces each) tomato sauce

1 can (29 ounces) diced tomatoes

2 tablespoons dried basil leaves

2 teaspoons salt, divided

½ teaspoon ground black pepper

1 package (12 ounces) whole wheat lasagna noodles

2 eggs

2 cups small curd cottage cheese

2 tablespoons dried Italian seasoning

½ cup grated Parmesan cheese

16 ounces shredded mozzarella cheese

1. Preheat the oven to 375°F. Coat a 13″ x 9″ baking dish with cooking spray.

2. In a large nonstick skillet, heat the oil over medium-high heat. Add the onion and garlic and cook, stirring frequently, until the onion begins to soften, about 5 minutes.

3. Add the ground beef and ground sausage and cook until no longer pink, breaking the meat up as it cooks. Drain and return to the pan.

4. Add the tomato sauce, diced tomatoes, basil, 1 teaspoon of the salt, and the pepper. Bring to a simmer, reduce the heat to low, and cook for 30 minutes.

5. Meanwhile, in a large stockpot, bring salted water to a boil and cook the pasta according to package directions. Drain.

6. While the pasta is cooking, in a medium mixing bowl, stir together the eggs, cottage cheese, Italian seasoning, the remaining 1 teaspoon salt, and the Parmesan. Set aside.

7. In the baking dish, lay out half of the lasagna noodles in a single layer. Follow with half of the cheese mixture, half of the meat sauce, and 2 cups of the mozzarella. Repeat each layer again, ending with the mozzarella on top. (*Freezing instructions begin here.*)

8. Bake for 30 minutes, or until golden brown on top and bubbly. Let it cool slightly before serving.

GOES WELL WITH

✓ Crowd Pleaser
   Green Beans
   (recipe available on
   Thriving Home)

✓ Garden salad

Freezer Meal Instructions

TO FREEZE: Assemble the lasagna completely, but do not bake. Wrap the dish tightly in several layers of plastic wrap and 1 or 2 layers of foil, squeeze out excess air, and freeze.

TO PREPARE FROM FROZEN: Thaw in the refrigerator for 24 hours. Set out on the counter for about 30 minutes to bring to room temperature, and then bake as directed.

Cooking Notes

▶ When baking, place a baking sheet on the rack below your baking dish to catch any overflow.

▶ You could make two 9″ x 9″ dishes instead of one 13″ x 9″. This would be an easy way to freeze one!

Sweet Potato and Black Bean Chili, *page 181*

soups

TOMATO BISQUE

Would you ever guess you'd want to lick the bowl and spoon clean of a bowl full of vegetables? Well, that's what you'll be doing every time you eat this hearty, comforting, and nutritious bisque. In the cooler months, I make this creamy soup regularly; one of these big batches makes enough to freeze half for another meal later. The fire-roasted tomatoes really make a difference in this recipe, but if you can't find them, plain diced tomatoes will still work. I highly recommend investing in an immersion blender, which isn't that pricey, to cut down on the mess. But a regular blender does the job. Serve with a whole grain grilled cheese sandwich on the side for a complete meal, and then send leftovers in lunches the next day. —RACHEL

Yield: 8–10 servings

¼ cup olive oil or avocado oil

2 medium onions, chopped

2 medium carrots, chopped

2 ribs celery, chopped

4 cloves garlic, chopped

Salt and ground black pepper

½ teaspoon red-pepper flakes, or to taste

6 tablespoons whole wheat flour

2 quarts vegetable or Chicken Broth (page 217)

2 cans (28 ounces each) diced fire-roasted tomatoes, drained (look for BPA-free cans)

6 tablespoons tomato paste

4 teaspoons sugar

½ cup half-and-half, or more to taste

¼ cup unsalted butter

Hot sauce, for serving

Freshly grated Parmesan cheese, for serving

1. In a large stockpot or Dutch oven, heat the oil over medium-high heat. Add the onions, carrots, celery, and garlic. Season lightly with salt and black pepper to taste, and add the red-pepper flakes. Cook, stirring occasionally, until the vegetables are just beginning to soften, about 5 minutes.

2. Sprinkle the flour over the vegetables and stir for 1 minute, or until the flour is fully incorporated. Add the broth, tomatoes, tomato paste, and sugar. Season lightly with additional salt and black pepper. Bring to a boil, then reduce the heat to a simmer and cover partially with a lid. Cook, stirring occasionally, until the vegetables are tender, about 15 minutes.

3. Allow the soup to cool slightly, then transfer the soup in batches to a blender or use an immersion blender in the pot and puree until fairly smooth. (*Note:* Please be careful during this step! Don't fill the blender entirely full. Cover the lid with a towel and hold securely while blending, so the lid doesn't pop off.) Carefully return the puree to the pot.

(CONTINUED)

GOES WELL WITH

✓ Turkey Pesto
   Paninis (page 129)
✓ Pesto and Feta
   Tuna Melts
   (page 147)

4. Reduce the heat to medium low. Stir in the half-and-half and cook until the soup is just heated through. Swirl in the butter. Taste and then season with salt, black pepper, and hot sauce to your preference. *(Freezing instructions begin here.)* Ladle the soup into bowls and garnish with freshly grated cheese.

Freezer Meal Instructions

TO FREEZE: Cook and cool completely. Freeze in a freezer bag or container, squeezing out all excess air and sealing tightly.

TO PREPARE FROM FROZEN: Thaw in the refrigerator and warm over medium-low heat, stirring occasionally.

Cooking Notes

▶ You don't have to worry too much about chopping the vegetables precisely, since the soup will be blended at the end.

BROCCOLI CHEDDAR POTATO SOUP

This one-pot wonder combines the flavor and texture of two of our favorite comfort soups: potato soup and broccoli cheddar soup. You can choose the consistency you prefer by blending part or none of it. It's really up to you. Serve with some crusty bread on a cold winter night for the perfect soul-warming dinner after a long day. *Yield: 6 servings*

4½ tablespoons butter, divided

1 small onion, diced

2 cloves garlic, minced

3 cups low-sodium vegetable or Chicken Broth (page 217)

3½ cups peeled, cubed russet potatoes

¼ teaspoon dried ground thyme

Salt and ground black pepper

4 cups finely chopped broccoli florets

¼ cup unbleached all-purpose flour

3½ cups whole milk

2 cups shredded Cheddar cheese

½ cup finely shredded Parmesan cheese

GOES WELL WITH

✓ Bread Machine Wheat Rolls (recipe available on Thriving Home)

1. In a large pot, melt 1½ tablespoons of the butter over medium-high heat. Add the onion and cook, stirring frequently, for about 4 minutes, or until translucent. Add the garlic and cook for 30 to 60 seconds.

2. Stir in the broth, potatoes, thyme, and salt and pepper to taste. Bring to a boil, then reduce the heat to a simmer. Partially cover the pot with a lid and cook for 15 minutes, stirring occasionally. Stir in the broccoli and cook for 5 minutes longer, or until the veggies are tender. Use an immersion blender or regular blender to blend half of the soup, if desired.

3. Meanwhile, in a medium saucepan, melt the remaining 3 tablespoons butter over medium heat. Stir in the flour and cook, whisking constantly, for 1 minute. Slowly pour in the milk while whisking. Increase the heat to medium high. Whisk until all lumps disappear and the mixture begins to gently simmer and thicken, 3 to 5 minutes. Stir into the soup.

4. Remove the soup from the heat and stir in the Cheddar and Parmesan until melted. Taste and adjust the seasoning, if needed. Serve warm. *(Freezing instructions begin here.)*

Freezer Meal Instructions

TO FREEZE: Cook and cool completely. Freeze in a freezer bag or container, squeezing out all excess air and sealing tightly.

TO PREPARE FROM FROZEN: Thaw in the refrigerator. Warm over medium-low heat, stirring occasionally. Add 1 to 2 more cups of chicken broth if too thick.

GOES WELL WITH

✓ Homemade Wheat Sandwich
   Bread (recipe available on
   Thriving Home)

CREAMY BUTTERNUT SQUASH SOUP

Recipe courtesy of Maureen Witmer of Take Them a Meal

This soup is one of my family's favorites. It's especially good in fall, but we enjoy it all year round. One of the reasons I love it is because it makes a ton, and we can save half to keep on hand for a friend in need. Butternut squash can be cumbersome to work with. Try making a few large slits in the squash with a knife, then microwave for 3 to 5 minutes and let cool. This will make it easier to peel and cut. —MAUREEN WITMER Yield: 10–12 servings

5 tablespoons butter

½ medium onion, chopped (¾–1 cup)

4 medium carrots, sliced (about 2 cups)

6 cups vegetable or Chicken Broth (page 217)

7 cups (about 3 pounds) peeled and cubed fresh or frozen butternut squash

3 medium zucchini, peeled and cubed (4–5 cups)

½ teaspoon dried thyme

1 teaspoon salt, plus more to taste

¼ teaspoon ground black pepper, plus more to taste

1 cup half-and-half

½ cup milk

Freshly grated Parmesan cheese, chopped chives, and roasted pumpkin seeds (optional, for topping)

1. In a large pot, melt the butter over medium-high heat just until bubbling (do not let it burn). Add the onion and carrots and cook, stirring occasionally, for about 5 minutes, or until softened.

2. Add the broth, squash, zucchini, thyme, salt, and pepper. Bring to a boil. Cover and reduce the heat. Simmer for 30 minutes, stirring occasionally.

3. Remove from the heat and cool slightly. Puree the soup in batches using a food processor, immersion blender, or regular blender until smooth. (*Note:* Cover the blender lid with a towel and hold firmly to prevent the lid from coming off.) Return the soup to the pot.

4. After the pureed soup has cooled slightly, stir in the half-and-half and milk and warm gently over medium-low heat (do not boil).

5. Taste and adjust the seasoning with additional salt and pepper, if needed. (*Freezing instructions begin here.*) Garnish each bowl with grated cheese, chives, or pumpkin seeds, if using.

Freezer Meal Instructions

TO FREEZE: Cook and cool the soup completely. Freeze in a freezer bag or container, squeezing out all excess air and sealing tightly.

TO PREPARE FROM FROZEN: Thaw in the refrigerator. Warm over medium-low heat, stirring occasionally.

Cooking Notes

▶ If you're having trouble finding the right size squash, feel free to use part butternut squash and part acorn squash. Just be sure to use about 7 cups total.

HEARTY VEGETABLE LENTIL SOUP

What better way to clean out your fridge and freezer than to make a satisfying pot of vegetable soup? I make a form of this at least once a month and then eat it all week long or freeze it for later. Sautéing the tomato paste along with the aromatics adds a bit of umami flavor to what can often be a boring broth. Now, let's talk lentils for a moment. Not only are these small dried seeds of a legume plant high in fiber, protein, and many other essential vitamins and minerals, but they also lend a mild-tasting creaminess as they "melt" into the soup. If you don't have lentils on hand, black beans or garbanzo beans are a good substitute.
—RACHEL Yield: 12–14 servings

2 tablespoons olive oil or avocado oil

1 large onion, diced (about 3 cups)

3 ribs celery, diced (about 1½ cups)

2 cups diced carrots

¼ teaspoon red-pepper flakes (or less for milder heat)

Salt and ground black pepper

3 cloves garlic, minced

2 tablespoons tomato paste

3 quarts (or three 32-ounce cartons) vegetable or Chicken Broth (page 217)

1 can (28 ounces) petite diced tomatoes (look for BPA-free cans)

1 cup red or green lentils, rinsed and sorted

1 medium zucchini, diced (3 cups)

1 pound green beans, trimmed and chopped (about 3 cups)

1 cup frozen corn

1½ cups frozen green peas

Freshly grated Parmesan cheese, for serving

1. In a large pot, heat the oil over medium-high heat just until the oil shimmers. Do not let it burn. Add the onion, celery, and carrots. Stir in the red-pepper flakes and season to taste with salt and black pepper. Cook, stirring frequently, until the vegetables are soft, about 6 minutes.

2. Add the garlic and tomato paste and cook, stirring, for 1 minute.

3. Stir in the broth, tomatoes (with juice), lentils, zucchini, green beans, and corn. Season well again with salt and black pepper. Increase the heat to high, bring to a boil, and then reduce the heat to a simmer. Cook for 20 to 25 minutes, stirring occasionally.

4. Reduce the heat to low and stir in the frozen peas. Taste and adjust the seasoning, if needed. *(Freezing instructions begin here.)*

5. Serve warm topped with grated cheese and crusty bread on the side.

(CONTINUED)

GOES WELL WITH

✓ Ham and Swiss
  Glazed Paninis
  (page 120)

✓ Pesto and Feta
  Tuna Melts
  (page 147)

Freezer Meal Instructions

TO FREEZE: Cook and cool the soup completely. Freeze in a freezer bag or container, squeezing out all excess air and sealing tightly.

TO PREPARE FROM FROZEN: Thaw in the refrigerator. Warm over medium-low heat, stirring occasionally.

Cooking Notes

▶ Try to dice the vegetables so they're about the same size and small enough to fit on a soup spoon.

▶ Feel free to substitute other vegetables in this recipe, such as chopped broccoli, cauliflower, summer squash, potatoes, mushrooms, tomatoes, winter greens, and peppers.

SWEET POTATO AND BLACK BEAN CHILI

Recipe courtesy of Camille Styles of CamilleStyles.com

This sweet potato and black bean chili has become my go-to dinner delivery for friends who need a little TLC. It's always a bit of a challenge to figure out what to take to new mamas or sick friends, or even to potluck gatherings. I'm always on the hunt for dishes that can be easily reheated, are packed with nutrition, and, most important, are incredibly delicious. This chili also fits a variety of dietary needs, which is important to me since several of my friends are either vegetarian or gluten-free. This recipe is all of the above and more. —CAMILLE STYLES

Yield: 8 servings

---

1 tablespoon olive oil

1 sweet potato, peeled and chopped

1 onion, chopped

1 red bell pepper, seeded and chopped

6 cloves garlic, minced

2 tablespoons tomato paste

2 tablespoons chili powder

1½ tablespoons ground cumin

Kosher salt and freshly ground black pepper

1 can (28 ounces) crushed tomatoes (I like to use fire-roasted)

2 cans (15 ounces each) black beans, drained and rinsed

1 tablespoon honey

2 cups water

Toppings: sliced avocado, crumbled goat cheese, sliced scallions, sliced radishes, tortilla chips

1. In a Dutch oven or large stockpot, heat the oil over medium-high heat. Add the sweet potato, onion, and bell pepper and cook, stirring occasionally, for 10 minutes.

2. Stir in the garlic, tomato paste, chili powder, cumin, and salt and black pepper to taste. Add the tomatoes, black beans, honey, and water. Bring to a simmer. Reduce the heat to low, cover, and cook for 30 minutes, or until the sweet potato is very tender.

3. Taste and adjust the seasoning, adding more salt and chili powder as needed. (*Freezing instructions begin here.*) Divide among bowls, add toppings, and eat!

Freezer Meal Instructions

TO FREEZE: Cook and cool completely. Freeze in a freezer bag or container, squeezing out all excess air and sealing tightly.

TO PREPARE FROM FROZEN: Thaw in the refrigerator, then warm over medium-low heat, stirring occasionally.

GOES WELL WITH
✓ Cornbread

CREAMY CHICKEN, VEGGIE, AND WILD RICE SOUP

Keep this recipe close for football weekends, when company comes, or just to enjoy on a cold winter night while watching your favorite movie. Be sure to read through the entire recipe and get set up before starting. It does require several steps and a bit of time and attention, but the end result is so worth it. —RACHEL Yield: 6 servings

---

8 tablespoons butter, divided

1 cup chopped yellow onion

1 cup diced celery

1 cup diced carrots

1½ teaspoons salt, divided, plus more to taste

¾ teaspoon ground black pepper, divided, plus more to taste

2 cloves garlic, minced

1 quart (32 ounces) store-bought or homemade Chicken Broth (page 217)

1 teaspoon poultry seasoning

1 pound boneless, skinless chicken breasts

½ cup whole wheat flour

2 cups whole milk

2 cups cooked wild rice blend

GOES WELL WITH

✓ Whole Wheat Buttermilk Biscuits (recipe available on Thriving Home)

1. In a large Dutch oven or pot, melt 1 tablespoon of the butter over medium-high heat. Add the onion, celery, carrots, ½ teaspoon of the salt, and ¼ teaspoon of the pepper. Cook, stirring frequently, just until the vegetables are tender, 4 to 5 minutes. Add the garlic for the last 30 to 60 seconds.

2. Stir in the broth, poultry seasoning, remaining 1 teaspoon salt, remaining ½ teaspoon pepper, and the chicken breasts. Bring to a boil and then reduce the heat to a simmer. Simmer for 12 to 15 minutes, or until the chicken is no longer pink inside, stirring the chicken breasts around occasionally for even cooking. Remove and set aside the chicken to a cutting board.

3. Meanwhile, in a medium pot, melt the remaining 7 tablespoons butter over medium heat. Stir in the flour and cook for 1 to 2 minutes, or until bubbly. Slowly pour in the milk while continually whisking. Increase the heat to medium-high and whisk constantly until the milk mixture thickens to the consistency of thin gravy, 3 to 5 minutes.

4. Add the milk mixture and prepared wild rice to the soup pot, stir, reduce the heat to medium low, and simmer. Shred the chicken using 2 forks or chop into bite-size pieces. Return to the pot and heat until warmed through, about 5 minutes. Taste and adjust the seasoning, if needed. *(Freezing instructions begin here.)*

Freezer Meal Instructions

TO FREEZE: Cook and cool the soup completely. Freeze in a freezer bag or container, squeezing out all excess air and sealing tightly.

TO PREPARE FROM FROZEN: Thaw in the refrigerator. Warm over medium-low heat, stirring occasionally. Add 1 to 2 more cups of chicken broth if too thick.

CLASSIC CHICKEN NOODLE SOUP

Homemade chicken noodle soup doesn't get much easier than this recipe. Find whole wheat egg noodles in the pasta aisle, or make your own using the 3-ingredient recipe on our blog, Thriving Home. By cooking the chicken directly in the soup, you save time and mess and add flavor to the broth at the same time. There are two tricks to successfully freezing this soup: (1) freeze it before adding the noodles; and (2) freeze the chicken separately from the broth, so that it doesn't get overcooked later when boiling the noodles. *Yield: 8 servings*

---

1 tablespoon butter

½ cup diced onion

1 rib celery, sliced

2 cups sliced carrots

¾ teaspoon kosher salt, divided

¼ teaspoon ground black pepper, divided

2 cloves garlic, minced

½ teaspoon ground thyme

2 quarts (64 ounces) store-bought or homemade Chicken Broth (page 217)

1–1½ pounds boneless, skinless chicken breasts, trimmed of excess fat

2 cups dried whole wheat egg noodles

1. In a large stockpot, heat the butter over medium-high heat just until it melts. Stir in the onion, celery, and carrots. Season with $\frac{1}{4}$ teaspoon salt and $\frac{1}{8}$ teaspoon pepper. Cook, stirring frequently, until the vegetables are soft, about 5 minutes. Add the garlic and thyme and cook, stirring, for 30 to 60 seconds, or until the garlic is fragrant.

2. Increase the heat to high. Stir in the broth, cover, and bring to a boil. Once boiling, remove the lid and add the chicken, $\frac{1}{2}$ teaspoon salt, and $\frac{1}{8}$ teaspoon pepper. Reduce the heat to a simmer and cook for 12 to 15 minutes, or until the chicken is no longer pink inside and a thermometer inserted in the center of a breast registers 165°F.

3. With tongs, transfer the chicken to a wooden cutting board. Chop into bite-size pieces or, using 2 forks, shred it. Set aside. *(Freezing instructions begin here.)*

4. Add the noodles to the soup. Stir and bring back to a boil. Cook for 8 to 10 minutes, or according to package directions. Return the chicken to the soup and stir until warmed through. Taste and adjust seasoning, as needed.

✓ Whole grain
  crackers

✓ Apple slices

Freezer Meal Instructions

TO FREEZE: After Step 3 is completed, remove the soup from the heat and let cool completely. Freeze in a freezer container or gallon-size freezer bag. Place the chicken in a small freezer bag, squeeze out all air before sealing, and freeze alongside the soup. Measure out 2 cups of dry noodles into a small freezer bag and store with the soup and chicken for easy preparation later.

TO PREPARE FROM FROZEN: Thaw the soup and chicken in the refrigerator or in the microwave using the defrost setting. Transfer the soup to a pot, bring to a boil, and continue with Step 4.

ITALIAN SAUSAGE AND TORTELLINI SOUP

This soup became a Freezer Club staple over the years because it was always a hit with our families. I love that it's chock full of vegetables. My husband loves that it's chock full of Italian sausage. And my kids love that it's chock full of cheese tortellini. Win-win-win!
—RACHEL *Yield: 8–10 servings*

---

1 pound all-natural mild Italian sausage, crumbled and cooked

1 teaspoon dried Italian seasoning

1 cup diced onions

2 cups diced carrots

1 cup diced celery

⅛ teaspoon red-pepper flakes, or more to taste

Salt and ground black pepper

3 cloves garlic, minced

2 cans (14 ounces each) non-marinated, quartered artichoke hearts

1 can (14 ounces) petite diced tomatoes

1 can (28 ounces) tomato sauce

2 quarts (64 ounces) store-bought or homemade Chicken Broth (page 217)

1 package (19 ounces) frozen all-natural cheese tortellini

4 cups packed baby spinach, roughly chopped

Freshly grated Parmesan cheese, for serving

1. In a large stockpot over medium-high heat, combine the sausage and Italian seasoning. Cook until no longer pink, about 5 minutes. Set aside on paper towels to drain.

2. Add the onions, carrots, celery, red-pepper flakes, and salt and black pepper to taste to the pot. Cook, stirring frequently, until soft, about 5 minutes. Add the garlic during the last 30 to 60 seconds of cooking time, so it doesn't burn.

3. Add the cooked sausage, the liquid from the artichoke hearts (reserve the artichokes), the tomatoes (including juice), tomato sauce, and broth, and stir to combine. Bring to a boil. While the soup comes to a boil, chop the artichokes into bite-size pieces and toss into the pot. Reduce the heat to a simmer and cook for 15 to 20 minutes. *(Freezing instructions begin here.)*

4. Add the tortellini and spinach. Cook according to the tortellini package directions. Taste and adjust the seasoning, if needed. Serve with cheese on top.

(CONTINUED)

GOES WELL WITH

✓ A salad with
  Balsamic Dressing
  with Herbs (recipe
  available on
  Thriving Home)

Freezer Meal Instructions

TO FREEZE: Stop cooking the soup at the end of Step 3, before adding the tortellini and spinach. Cool completely and freeze in a freezer bag or container, squeezing out all excess air and sealing tightly.

TO PREPARE FROM FROZEN: Thaw the soup in the refrigerator or in the microwave in a glass bowl using the defrost setting. Then bring to a simmer in a stockpot on the stove. Add the tortellini and spinach and cook according to package directions. Serve as directed.

Cooking Notes

▶ If you can't find all-natural tortellini in the health food section, be sure to read the labels of any other options and choose the one with the fewest ingredients in it.

▶ Want more heat? Use hot Italian sausage instead of mild or add more red-pepper flakes.

▶ If you have a family who may not go for the artichokes, try using 1 can instead of 2.

CHEESEBURGER SOUP

Here's a fun dinner idea that everyone will love: cheeseburgers ... as a soup! This hearty one-pot wonder makes even the coldest winter nights warm and cozy. For a change, try cooked, shredded chicken or ground turkey in place of the ground beef. Either one works great! Serve for a weeknight meal or at your next group gathering. *Yield: 8 servings*

½ pound lean ground beef

1½ teaspoons salt, divided

½ teaspoon ground black pepper, divided

½ teaspoon garlic powder

½ teaspoon dried Italian seasoning

4 tablespoons butter, divided

¾ cup chopped onion (about 1 small onion)

¾ cup chopped celery

¾ cup chopped carrots

2 cloves garlic, minced

3 cups store-bought or homemade Chicken Broth (page 217)

1½ teaspoons dried basil

4 cups peeled, diced potatoes (about 1¾ pounds)

¼ cup whole wheat flour

1½ cups whole milk

8 ounces sharp Cheddar cheese, shredded

1. In a large nonstick skillet over medium-high heat, add the beef, ½ teaspoon of the salt, ¼ teaspoon of the pepper, the garlic powder, and Italian seasoning. Cook, stirring, until the meat is no longer pink. Drain and transfer the meat to a large stockpot. Set aside.

2. In the same skillet, melt 1 tablespoon of the butter. Add the onion, celery, carrots, and garlic. Cook, stirring, for 8 to 10 minutes, or until the vegetables are tender.

3. Transfer the vegetables to the stockpot and stir in the broth, basil, and potatoes. Bring to a boil. Reduce the heat to medium low and cover. Simmer for 10 to 12 minutes, or until the potatoes are tender.

4. Wipe out the skillet and melt the remaining 3 tablespoons butter over medium heat. Add the flour and stir for 3 to 5 minutes, or until bubbly. Stir the butter and flour mixture into the soup and bring to a boil. Cook for 2 minutes.

5. Reduce the heat to low. Add the milk, remaining 1 teaspoon salt, and remaining ¼ teaspoon pepper. Slowly stir in the cheese and cook until melted. *(Freezing instructions begin here.)*

Freezer Meal Instructions

TO FREEZE: Cook and cool the soup completely. Freeze in a freezer bag or container.

TO PREPARE FROM FROZEN: Thaw in the refrigerator or using the defrost setting of the microwave. Warm over medium-low heat, stirring occasionally.

Killer Carnitas, *page 196*

slow cooker meals

CHICKEN AND CHEESE CHIMICHANGAS

Our recipe testing team went gaga over these chimichangas! We tweaked the classic deep-fried Tex-Mex favorite, making it quite a bit simpler (and a little less fried). Thanks to the good ol' slow cooker, the chicken filling is infused with Mexican flavors and creamy cheese. To give the chimichangas their signature crispy tortilla crust, we opted for a quick, shallow pan-fry. These work well to cook ahead of time and reheat for on-the-go lunches.

Yield: 6–8 chimichangas

1 pound chicken breasts

2 tablespoons all-natural taco seasoning

¾ cup store-bought or homemade Chicken Broth (page 217)

¼ cup cream cheese

¼ cup all-natural salsa

¼ cup whole wheat flour

¼ cup water

6–8 burrito-size whole wheat tortillas (10" diameter)

½ cup vegetable oil or avocado oil, divided (for shallow frying)

Sour cream, salsa, guacamole, and shredded lettuce (optional, for topping)

1. Rub both sides of the chicken breasts with the taco seasoning and place in a slow cooker. Add the broth. Cover and cook on low for 3 to 4 hours, or until the chicken shreds easily.

2. Using 2 forks, shred the chicken in the slow cooker. If there is any excess liquid in the slow cooker, remove it. Add the cream cheese and salsa, and gently stir until the cream cheese is melted.

3. In a small bowl, mix the flour and water together to make the "glue" that will hold the tortillas shut.

4. Warm up the tortillas in the microwave for about 30 seconds, so they are easy to work with without tearing. Scoop about ½ cup of the chicken mixture and place in the middle of a tortilla. Fold the sides of the tortilla in toward each other so they overlap a bit. Then fold the top and the bottom, sealing off the opening to the chicken mixture. This will create a square-shaped chimichanga. Spread the flour paste under each of the overlapping parts of the tortilla to secure the flaps in place. Repeat with the remaining tortillas and chicken mixture. (*Freezing instructions begin here.*)

5. In a large skillet, heat ¼ cup of the oil over medium heat. (The oil should be hot enough to make the chimichangas sizzle when they're placed in the pan!) Place a few of the chimichangas folded side down in the pan, making sure they do not touch. Cook for 2 to 4 minutes, turning once, or until the tortilla is golden brown on both sides. Repeat with the rest of the chimichangas and add oil as needed.

6. Serve warm with your favorite toppings.

(CONTINUED)

✓ Guacamole (recipe available on Thriving Home)

✓ Grilled corn on the cob (instructions available on Thriving Home)

Freezer Meal Instructions

TO FREEZE: Place the assembled chimichangas in an airtight freezer container or bag and separate layers with parchment paper. Freeze.

TO PREPARE FROM FROZEN: Let thaw in the refrigerator for 24 hours. Cook as directed.

Cooking Notes

▶ It can sometimes be hard to find large whole wheat tortillas. I suggest looking at your local health food store. If you can find only medium ones, just decrease the amount of chicken in each chimichanga to $1/3$ cup.

▶ If cooking 1 chimichanga at a time, use about 1 to 2 tablespoons of oil per chimichanga.

▶ When adding the cream cheese and salsa to the cooked chicken, feel free to also add pinto beans (rinsed and drained), chopped mild green chiles, or chipotle chiles.

CHILI-RUBBED BEEF BRISKET

Some people prefer a choice steak, but beef brisket is the king of cuts in our opinion. After a long chill in a complex rub mix, this brisket cooks low and slow all day long. The road to a perfect brisket isn't hard, but you do have to be patient. The wait is worth it when this tender, fall-apart cut makes it to your plate. When brisket goes on sale, be sure to double up and freeze one in the rub seasoning for later. *Yield: 8–10 servings*

2 tablespoons kosher salt

2 tablespoons dark brown sugar

1 tablespoon garlic powder

1 tablespoon onion powder

1 tablespoon Spanish paprika

1 tablespoon chili powder

1½ teaspoons freshly ground black pepper

½ teaspoon ground cayenne pepper

½ teaspoon celery seed

1 flat-cut brisket (4–5 pounds)

1 cup apple juice

1½ cups your favorite all-natural barbecue sauce, for serving

8–10 whole wheat hamburger buns (optional)

1. In a small bowl, mix together the salt, brown sugar, garlic powder, onion powder, paprika, chili powder, black pepper, cayenne pepper, and celery seed until well combined.

2. Pat the brisket dry with paper towels. Rub the dry seasoning mix into all sides and crevices of the brisket. (*Note:* There may be extra rub, but just make sure every part of the surface is covered well.) (*Freezing instructions begin here.*) Tightly wrap the brisket in a few layers of plastic wrap, place on a rimmed baking sheet (to catch any drips), and refrigerate for 24 hours.

3. Place the unwrapped brisket in a 6-quart slow cooker and pour the apple juice over the top. Cover and cook on low for about 8 hours. Shred the meat in the slow cooker using tongs or 2 forks.

4. Serve with some of the defatted au jus on top and/or your favorite barbecue sauce, either on buns or as a main dish.

Freezer Meal Instructions

TO FREEZE: Rub the brisket with the seasoning mixture. Wrap tightly in several layers of plastic wrap and 1 or 2 layers of foil. Freeze.

TO PREPARE FROM FROZEN: Thaw completely in the refrigerator on a rimmed baking sheet for 24 to 48 hours. Cook according to the directions in Step 3.

GOES WELL WITH

✓ Super Stuffed Baked Potatoes (page 121)

✓ Asian Slaw (recipe available on Thriving Home)

KILLER CARNITAS

"**W**oman, what have you done?!" This was my husband's affectionate way of telling me he was a big fan of this recipe. After cooking it for 8 hours in the slow cooker, you'll be left with fall-apart, flavorful chunks of juicy pork that you can then broil for a few minutes in order to give some extra texture. Wrap up the meat in a soft tortilla and top it with cheese, avocados, diced red onions, lime juice, cilantro, or whatever Mexican toppings you prefer, and you'll be going loco over these carnitas. Not much work for a whole lot of goodness. —**POLLY**

Yield: 8 servings

---

1 teaspoon ground oregano

2 teaspoons ground cumin

1 teaspoon chili powder

2 teaspoons salt

1 teaspoon ground black pepper

4–5 pounds pork shoulder (also known as pork butt or Boston butt)

¼ cup lime juice

½ cup orange juice

1 tablespoon hot sauce

5 cloves garlic, minced

1 medium white or yellow onion, diced

GOES WELL WITH

✓ Avocado Lime Salsa (recipe available on Thriving Home)

✓ Roasted Corn and Black Bean Salsa (recipe available on Thriving Home)

1. In a small bowl, mix together the oregano, cumin, chili powder, salt, and pepper. Using your hands, rub the seasonings into the pork. *(Freezing instructions begin here.)* Place the seasoned pork in a 6-quart slow cooker.

2. In a medium bowl, mix together the lime juice, orange juice, hot sauce, garlic, and onion. Pour over the meat.

3. Cover and cook on low for 6 to 8 hours or on high for 4 to 5 hours, or until the pork is tender and easily pulled apart.

4. Preheat the broiler. Remove the pork from the slow cooker and place on a foil-lined baking sheet. Using 2 forks, pull apart the meat into small chunks.

5. Broil the meat for 3 minutes. Using tongs, turn the meat over and spoon about ¼ cup of the juices from the slow cooker over the meat. Broil another 3 to 4 minutes, or until the edges of the meat start to crisp up and turn brown. Remove from the oven and spoon another ¼ cup of the juices over the cooked pork.

6. Serve immediately in tacos, burritos, or salads, or enjoy plain.

Freezer Meal Instructions

TO FREEZE: Place the seasoned pork and marinade from Step 2 in a gallon-size freezer bag. Squeeze out all excess air, seal tightly, and freeze.

TO PREPARE FROM FROZEN: Let the pork thaw in the refrigerator for 24 hours, or more if needed. Cook as directed.

FRENCH DIP SANDWICHES

This meal ranks up there with good ole tacos and spaghetti in terms of being a crowd-pleaser in my house. I love that I can throw all the ingredients in the slow cooker first thing in the morning and come home 8 to 10 hours later to a house that smells divine and a dinner that's ready to go. —RACHEL *Yield: 8–12 servings*

1 boneless beef roast (2–3 pounds), trimmed of excess fat

1 large onion, halved and thinly sliced

4 cloves garlic, minced

1 bay leaf

3 cups reduced-sodium beef or chicken broth

2 tablespoons lower-sodium soy sauce

2 tablespoons Worcestershire sauce

1 teaspoon ground black pepper

1 teaspoon onion powder

1 teaspoon dried oregano, crushed in hand

1 teaspoon ground thyme

8–12 whole grain ciabatta rolls

8–12 slices Provolone cheese

1. *(Freezing instructions for Method 1 begin here.)* Place the roast, onion, garlic, and bay leaf in a 6-quart slow cooker.

2. In a small mixing bowl, stir together the broth, soy sauce, Worcestershire sauce, pepper, onion powder, oregano, and thyme. Pour over the roast and cover.

3. Cook on low for 8 to 10 hours, or until the meat shreds easily. Remove the bay leaf. Shred the meat with 2 forks in the slow cooker. *(Freezing instructions for Method 2 begin here.)*

4. Preheat the broiler. Place the bottoms of the ciabatta rolls on a sheet pan with the cut side facing up, setting the tops aside. Top with meat and a slice of cheese. Broil for about 2 minutes, or until the cheese is melted. Cover with the tops of the rolls.

5. Alongside the sandwiches, ladle about $\frac{1}{3}$ cup of au jus (the leftover juices in the slow cooker) for each person in a small bowl for dipping.

Freezer Meal Instructions

TO FREEZE

METHOD 1: Place the broth, soy sauce, Worcestershire sauce, pepper, onion powder, oregano, and thyme in a gallon-size freezer bag. Seal and shake to combine. Then add the roast, onion, garlic, and bay leaf. Seal, squeeze out excess air, and toss to combine. Freeze the packages of rolls and cheese next to the meat in the freezer.

METHOD 2: Cook the roast and let cool completely. Freeze the shredded meat in the au jus in a large freezer container or bag. Freeze the packages of rolls and cheese next to the meat in the freezer.

TO PREPARE FROM FROZEN

METHOD 1: Thaw in the refrigerator or microwave using the defrost setting. Cook according to the recipe directions, starting with Step 3.

METHOD 2: Thaw in the refrigerator or microwave using the defrost setting. Reheat the meat in the juice on the stovetop over medium-low heat. Broil the sandwiches according to Step 4 and serve as suggested.

GOES WELL WITH

✓ Oven Fries with a Secret Ingredient (recipe available on Thriving Home)

✓ Steamed French-cut green beans

RACHEL'S FAVORITE POT ROAST

Guests at our home are probably familiar with this pot roast, because it's my go-to when we entertain. My favorite roast recipe from the past included a brown gravy packet mix and an Italian dressing packet mix, which are loaded with MSG, sodium, and a whole host of ingredients I can't pronounce. But this pot roast contains all whole food ingredients and has been tested and approved many times over. Plus, after a day of this in your slow cooker, your house will smell like home! —RACHEL Yield: 8–10 servings

---

2 tablespoons olive oil or avocado oil

1 beef chuck roast (2–3 pounds), trimmed of excess fat

Kosher salt and freshly ground black pepper

2 onions, diced

4 ribs celery, chopped

3 cloves garlic, minced

1 can (8 ounces) no-salt tomato sauce

¼ cup red wine

1 cup low-sodium chicken or beef broth

2 tablespoons whole wheat flour

2 fresh thyme sprigs or ½ teaspoon dried

1 bay leaf

4–5 large carrots, chopped into 1" pieces (about 3 cups)

4 medium russet potatoes, peeled and chopped into 1" pieces (about 5 cups)

1. In a medium mixing bowl, whisk together the tomato sauce, wine, broth, flour, and 1 teaspoon salt. Set aside. (*Freezing instructions for Method 1 begin here.*)

2. In a large skillet, heat the oil over medium-high heat. Season the roast on all sides with salt and pepper and then brown on all sides in the skillet, about 2 minutes per side. Place the roast in a 6-quart slow cooker.

3. In the same pan, cook the onions and celery, stirring frequently, until tender, about 4 to 5 minutes. Add the garlic and cook for 1 minute. Be sure to use a wooden spoon to scrape up the brown bits on the bottom of the pan, as this adds flavor.

4. Add the vegetable mixture to the slow cooker on top of the meat. Pour the sauce over the meat and veggies. Add the thyme and bay leaf and cover with the lid.

5. Cook on low for 5 to 6 hours. Add the carrots and potatoes and cook on low, covered, for another 3 to 4 hours, or until the vegetables are tender and the meat shreds easily. (*Note:* Total cooking time is 8 to 10 hours.)

6. Remove the bay leaf and any leftover thyme stems. Shred the meat using 2 forks in the slow cooker and gently stir. Taste and adjust the seasoning, if needed. (*Freezing instructions for Method 2 begin here.*)

(CONTINUED)

GOES WELL WITH

✓ Bread Machine
   Wheat Rolls (recipe
   available on
   Thriving Home)

✓ Salad with Honey
   Dijon Vinaigrette
   Salad Dressing
   (recipe available on
   Thriving Home)

Freezer Meal Instructions

TO FREEZE

METHOD 1: Complete Step 3, sautéing the onion, celery, and garlic. Set aside and let cool. Add tomato sauce, red wine, broth, flour, thyme, and bay leaf to a gallon-size freezer bag. Seal and shake to combine. Add the cooled vegetables to the bag. Season the roast with salt and pepper on all sides and add to the bag. Seal and freeze.

METHOD 2: Fully cook, shred, and cool the pot roast. Place in a gallon-size freezer bag or freezer container. Try to remove as much air as possible and seal and/or wrap it well before placing in the freezer.

TO PREPARE FROM FROZEN

METHOD 1: Dump the contents of the freezer bag into a 6-quart slow cooker. Follow Steps 5 and 6.

METHOD 2: Thaw for 24 to 48 hours in the refrigerator (preferred method) or in the microwave using the defrost setting. Then warm in the microwave or over low to medium-low heat on the stove, gently stirring occasionally. Add more broth if too thick.

CURT'S SLOW COOKER JAMBALAYA

My dad, Curt, has been making and honing this "dump and slow cook" Cajun specialty for quite some time. Let me tell you, he knocked it out of the park with this recipe! I love how easy it is to double the recipe and put half into a freezer bag for another meal, another time. Now, my parents like a lot of heat, so Dad usually adds 2 teaspoons (!!) of cayenne pepper to the dish. For my sensitive palate, that's way too much. So, in this adaptation, I omitted his usual cayenne and instead offer the suggestion to use hot sauce at the end to adjust the spice level for individual eaters. —RACHEL Yield: 8 servings

1–1¼ pounds boneless, skinless chicken breasts, cut into 1" cubes

12–14 ounces precooked, all-natural andouille sausage, thickly sliced

1 large onion, finely chopped

2 green bell peppers, finely chopped

1 cup finely chopped celery

1 can (28 ounces) petite diced tomatoes

1 cup store-bought or homemade Chicken Broth (page 217)

1 tablespoon Cajun seasoning (recommended: Tony Chachere's Creole Seasoning)

1 tablespoon dried oregano

2 teaspoons dried parsley

1 teaspoon dried thyme

8 cups cooked brown rice

Hot sauce (optional)

1. *(Freezing instructions begin here.)* In a 6-quart slow cooker, combine the chicken, sausage, onion, peppers, celery, tomatoes (with juice), broth, Cajun seasoning, oregano, parsley, and thyme. Cover and cook on high for 3 to 4 hours or on low for 5 to 6 hours. Do not overcook.

2. Serve over the rice. Taste and adjust the heat with hot sauce, if desired.

Freezer Meal Instructions

TO FREEZE: Combine all of the ingredients, except the brown rice and hot sauce, in a gallon-size freezer bag, press out all air, and seal well. Toss to make sure the liquid coats all of the ingredients and freeze.

TO PREPARE FROM FROZEN: Thaw in a dish (in case the bag leaks) in the refrigerator for 24 to 48 hours. Follow the cooking instructions starting with Step 1. Plan to cook for the longer time period, since the ingredients will be cold at the start.

CHICKEN PARMESAN SLIDERS

"I need more recipes like this in my life," I told my husband as he and the kids scarfed down slider after slider. When I can just dump a few ingredients in a slow cooker and then a healthy and kid-friendly meal magically appears at dinner time . . . *I'm in!* You can even freeze the leftovers and use them another time. —RACHEL *Yield: 12 sliders (6 servings)*

1½–1¾ pounds fresh or frozen boneless, skinless chicken breasts

1 jar (28 ounces) all-natural marinara sauce (or 3½ cups Slow Cooker Marinara Sauce, page 212)

12 mini wheat buns or dinner rolls

¾ cup freshly grated Parmesan cheese

6 slices provolone or mozzarella cheese, cut into fourths

GOES WELL WITH
✓ Oven Roasted Broccoli (recipe available on Thriving Home)
✓ Fruit salad

1. *(Freezing instructions for Method 1 begin here.)* Add the chicken breasts and marinara sauce to the slow cooker. Cook on low for 3 to 4 hours. The chicken is done when it shreds easily and is no longer pink.

2. Using 2 forks, shred the chicken and stir it into the sauce. *(Freezing instructions for Method 2 begin here.)*

3. To build a sandwich, place some hot shredded chicken inside a bun, sprinkle with about 1 tablespoon of Parmesan cheese, top with 2 cut-up pieces of provolone, and pop the top of the bun in place.

Freezer Meal Instructions

TO FREEZE
METHOD 1: Place the chicken and marinara sauce in a gallon-size freezer bag. Squeeze out excess air and seal. Freeze the packages of rolls and cheese with the chicken in the freezer.

METHOD 2: Fully cook, shred, and cool the chicken. Place in a freezer-safe container or gallon-size freezer bag. Squeeze out excess air and seal. Freeze the packages of rolls and cheese with the chicken in the freezer.

TO PREPARE FROM FROZEN
METHOD 1: Thaw everything in the refrigerator for 24 to 48 hours. Cook according to the recipe directions, starting with Step 1.

METHOD 2: Thaw everything in the refrigerator for 24 to 48 hours. Warm the chicken mixture over medium-low heat on the stove, stirring occasionally, in a slow cooker on low setting, or in the microwave. Serve according to the instructions in Step 3.

SLOW COOKER
SWEET AND SPICY CHICKEN

Recipe courtesy of Kelly Smith from The Nourishing Home

Transforming a classic take-out dish into a healthier and tastier home-cooked meal couldn't be easier! The all-natural sweetness of apricot jam combined with a flavorful array of seasonings results in a sweet-and-spicy sauce perfect with slow-cooked chicken, rice, and your favorite veggies. —KELLY SMITH *Yield: 6 servings*

---

3 pounds boneless, skinless chicken thighs

1 cup diced red bell pepper

2 cups all-fruit apricot jam

2 cloves garlic, minced

2 tablespoons gluten-free soy sauce or coconut aminos

2 tablespoons dry mustard

2 tablespoons dried minced onion

2 tablespoons sea salt

½ teaspoon ground ginger

½ teaspoon red-pepper flakes (or more for a spicier sauce)

2 tablespoons arrowroot powder (optional)

1. *(Freezing instructions begin here.)* Cut the chicken thighs into bite-size pieces and place in a 6-quart slow cooker. Top with the bell pepper.

2. In a medium bowl, whisk together the apricot jam, garlic, soy sauce or coconut aminos, mustard, onion, salt, ginger, and red-pepper flakes. Pour over the chicken and bell pepper.

3. Cover and cook on low for 5 to 6 hours. *(Since slow cookers vary in temperature, it's best to check this at the 5-hour mark. If the chicken is cooked through, it's ready to serve.)*

4. When ready to serve, use a slotted spoon to remove the chicken from the slow cooker and place in a serving dish. Whisk in the arrowroot powder to thicken the sauce, if desired. Ladle the sauce over the chicken and serve with your favorite veggies.

Freezer Meal Instructions

TO FREEZE: Place the chopped chicken and diced bell pepper in a freezer-safe container. Whisk together the sauce, add it to the container, and freeze.

TO PREPARE FROM FROZEN: Thaw the chicken mixture in the refrigerator for about 24 hours, or use the microwave defrost setting and stir occasionally for quick thawing. Follow the cooking instructions beginning in Step 3. Easy and delicious!

POLLY'S SIGNATURE TACO SOUP

I've been making a variation of this soup for my family for years. It's my go-to large group meal because crowds love it, too. It can be made in the slow cooker or on the stove and is fairly inexpensive. Lastly, it makes a very large batch, so we have lots of leftovers for the week or to freeze. —POLLY Yield: about 12 servings

2 tablespoons olive oil or avocado oil

1 yellow onion, diced

Salt and ground black pepper

3 cloves garlic, minced

2 pounds lean ground beef or ground turkey

¼ cup taco seasoning

1 can (15 ounces) black beans, rinsed and drained

1 can (15 ounces) pinto beans, rinsed and drained

1 can (28 ounces) petite diced tomatoes

1 can (4 ounces) diced green chiles

2 cans (11 ounces each) white shoepeg corn, drained

1 cup all-natural mild salsa

1 quart store-bought or homemade Chicken Broth (page 217)

Sour cream or plain Greek yogurt, shredded Cheddar cheese, sliced scallions, or tortilla chips, for topping (optional)

1. In a skillet, heat the oil over medium-high heat. Add the onion and cook until it begins to soften, about 5 minutes. Season lightly with salt and pepper. Stir in the garlic at the end and cook for 30 to 60 seconds, making sure not to burn it.

2. Add the beef or turkey and taco seasoning. Break up the meat with a wooden spoon and cook, stirring, until no longer pink. Drain any excess grease.

3. In either a 6-quart slow cooker or a large stockpot, combine the black beans, pinto beans, tomatoes (with juice), chiles (with liquid), corn, salsa, and chicken broth. Add the meat mixture and stir until well combined. (*Freezing instructions begin here.*)

4. Either cook on low for 6 to 8 hours in the slow cooker or simmer for 1 to 2 hours on the stove in the stockpot. Taste and adjust the seasoning, adding more salt and pepper to taste.

5. Serve in bowls with your favorite toppings.

Freezer Meal Instructions

TO FREEZE: Complete the recipe through Step 3, combining everything in a large bowl. Pour the uncooked soup into 2 gallon-size freezer bags or a large freezer container, seal tightly, and freeze.

TO PREPARE FROM FROZEN: Let the soup thaw for 24 hours (or more, if needed) in the fridge or run the bags under cool water until thawed. Cook as directed.

GOES WELL WITH
✓ Cornbread

freezer staples

SLOW COOKER MARINARA SAUCE

Once you realize how easy it is to make homemade marinara sauce, you'll never go back to the store-bought stuff again. When making it yourself, you can adjust the flavor according to your taste, and you are in total control of the ingredients. One batch will stock your freezer with multiple jars of sauce to pull out for many recipes in this book. Oh, and an extra bonus: When cooking, it makes your house smell ah-maz-ing!

Yield: about 4 quarts (16 cups)

¼ cup olive oil

2 large onions, diced

1 tablespoon finely chopped garlic

4 cans (28 ounces each) crushed tomatoes

1 tablespoon salt

⅓ cup chopped fresh basil or 2 tablespoons dried

3 tablespoons chopped fresh parsley or 1 tablespoon dried

½ teaspoon red-pepper flakes

1. In a large skillet, heat the olive oil over medium heat.

2. Add the onions and cook until softened, about 5 minutes. Add the garlic and stir for 30 to 60 seconds.

3. Transfer the onion mixture to a slow cooker and add the tomatoes, salt, basil, parsley, and red-pepper flakes.

4. Cover and cook on low for at least 4 hours. Adjust seasonings to taste.

Freezer Meal Instructions

TO FREEZE: Let the sauce cool and divide it among either freezer-safe Mason jars or freezer bags. If using jars, be sure to leave at least 1″ of headspace at the top of the jars. Freeze.

TO PREPARE FROM FROZEN: Either let the sauce thaw in the refrigerator for 24 hours or microwave on the defrost setting until it has thawed.

Cooking Note

▸ Add 1 cup of water if you prefer a thinner sauce.

Recipes That Use This Freezer Staple

▸ Chicken Parmesan Casserole *(page 71)*

▸ Family Favorite Baked Meatballs *(page 96)*

▸ Pesto Chicken Lasagna Rolls *(page 166)*

▸ Chicken Parmesan Sliders *(page 205)*

PIZZA SAUCE

This is one of those freezer staples that's super easy to make for meals like the Cheesy Lasagna Pockets or Make-Your-Own Calzones and to freeze for later, too. For a shortcut, buy pureed tomatoes and skip the food processing step. Yield: 2–3 cups

1 can (28 ounces) whole peeled tomatoes (recommended: Muir Glen Organic San Marzano)

2 tablespoons olive oil

2 large cloves garlic, minced

1 teaspoon sugar

½ teaspoon dried oregano, crushed in hand

½ teaspoon dried basil, crushed in hand

Salt and ground black pepper

1. Place the tomatoes in a food processor or blender and process or blend until smooth.

2. In a medium saucepan, heat the oil over medium heat. Once the oil is shimmering and hot, add the garlic and stir for about 1 minute, or just until it starts to turn golden. Be careful not to burn the garlic. Stir in the tomatoes (juice and all), sugar, oregano, and basil. Season lightly with salt and pepper.

3. Bring to a simmer and cook, uncovered, stirring occasionally, until the sauce thickens enough to coat a wooden spoon, about 30 minutes or more.

4. Taste and adjust the salt and pepper, if needed. Completely cool and store in the refrigerator for up to 2 weeks or in the freezer.

Freezer Meal Instructions

TO FREEZE: Complete the recipe through Step 4. Let the sauce cool completely. Measure out ½-cup increments into muffin pans and place in the freezer, uncovered, until frozen, 3 to 4 hours. Pop the sauce out of the muffin pans and place in a gallon-size freezer bag. Another option is to freeze the sauce in wide-mouthed, freezer-safe Mason jars. Be sure to leave at least 1″ of headspace at the top of the jars.

TO PREPARE FROM FROZEN: Thaw small portions of sauce in a bowl in the refrigerator for about 3 hours, or use the defrost setting of the microwave, stirring occasionally, until warmed through.

Recipes That Use This Freezer Staple

▸ English Muffin Pizzas (*page 160*)

▸ Cheesy Lasagna Pockets (*page 161*)

▸ Make-Your-Own Calzones (*page 164*)

PESTO

As we were developing recipes for this cookbook, we constantly gravitated toward anything with pesto in it. That's probably because of its big, fresh flavor that freezes well. The fresher, the better, too. Homemade pesto simply cannot be replicated! It is totally worth the time to stock up your freezer when basil is in season. *Yield: 1–1½ cups*

---

2 cups packed fresh basil leaves

2 cloves garlic, peeled

¼ cup pine nuts or walnuts

½ cup freshly grated Parmesan cheese

⅔ cup extra-virgin olive oil, divided

Kosher salt and freshly ground black pepper

1. In a food processor, combine the basil, garlic, nuts, and cheese. Pulse until coarsely chopped.

2. Add ½ cup of the olive oil and process until fully incorporated and smooth. Season with salt and pepper to taste.

Freezer Meal Instructions

TO FREEZE: Transfer the pesto to an airtight freezer container and drizzle the remaining olive oil over the top to prevent browning. Seal tightly with a lid and freeze. Or pour pesto into an ice cube tray, drizzle with the remaining oil, and freeze. Once frozen, transfer cubes to a freezer bag.

TO PREPARE FROM FROZEN: Let the pesto thaw in the refrigerator.

Recipes That Use This Freezer Staple
- ▶ Turkey Pesto Paninis *(page 129)*
- ▶ Pesto and Feta Tuna Melts *(page 147)*
- ▶ Chicken Pesto Pizza *(page 158)*
- ▶ Pesto Chicken Lasagna Rolls *(page 166)*

WHOLE WHEAT PIZZA DOUGH

Pizza dough is so easy and cheap to make at home. The secret to a light, nutty-tasting whole wheat dough is using the white whole wheat flour variety, which is now available in most major grocery stores. If you can't find that specific kind of flour, then use half whole wheat and half unbleached, all-purpose flour instead. Double this recipe and have dough on hand anytime! Yield: enough to make one 16" (large) pizza

1 cup warm water (110°F)

2¼ teaspoons active dry yeast

1 teaspoon sugar

1 tablespoon olive oil

1 tablespoon honey

1½ teaspoons salt

2½ cups white whole wheat flour (or 1¼ cups whole wheat flour and 1¼ cups unbleached all-purpose flour)

1. In the bowl of a stand mixer, combine the warm water, yeast, and sugar. Stir and let sit until the yeast starts to foam and bubble, 5 to 7 minutes.

2. Add the olive oil, honey, and salt to the bowl and stir. Using the dough hook, turn the mixer on low and add the flour in 1-cup increments until all is added. Once a dough starts to form, increase the speed to medium. If the dough is too sticky, add a little more flour. Mix for 5 minutes, or until the dough is well combined. Scrape down the sides halfway through the mixing time.

3. Dust the counter or another work surface with flour. Remove the dough and knead on the counter a few times and then form a ball. Place the dough ball in a well-greased bowl, cover loosely with a towel, and let rise for 30 minutes in a warm place. At this point, the dough is ready to use for calzones or pizza or to freeze for later use. If you want to use it later, wrap it in plastic wrap and refrigerate for 2 to 3 days.

Freezer Meal Instructions

TO FREEZE: After completing Step 3, place in the freezer in a freezer bag, making sure to squeeze out all excess air before sealing.

TO PREPARE FROM FROZEN: Thaw the dough in the refrigerator completely. Use within 2 to 3 days.

Recipes That Use This Freezer Staple
▶ Chicken Pesto Pizza *(page 158)*
▶ Cheesy Lasagna Pockets *(page 161)*
▶ Make-Your-Own Calzones *(page 164)*

CREAM OF CHICKEN SOUP

For years I felt a slave to buying cream of whatever soups at the store, even though I knew they were full of additives, preservatives, excess salt, and sugar. But I learned that making your own homemade version is super simple and even freezable! You can double this recipe, freeze in 1¼-cup increments (the same amount as one 10½-ounce can), and always be prepared for recipes that call for almost any cream soup. —RACHEL

Yield: about 2½ cups (equivalent of two 10½-ounce store-bought cans)

¼ cup unsalted butter

6 tablespoons unbleached all-purpose flour

2 cups store-bought or homemade Chicken Broth (page 217)

½ teaspoon salt, plus more to taste

¼ teaspoon ground black pepper, plus more to taste

½ teaspoon garlic powder

½ teaspoon onion powder

1 teaspoon dried parsley flakes, crushed in hand

¼ teaspoon ground thyme

¼ teaspoon ground sage

1 cup milk

1. In a medium saucepan, melt the butter over medium heat. Whisk in the flour and cook for about 2 minutes.

2. Add the broth, salt, pepper, garlic powder, onion powder, parsley, thyme, and sage. Whisk until there are no more lumps. Bring to a boil while whisking. Reduce the heat to a simmer.

3. Whisk in the milk and cook, stirring frequently, until thickened, 10 to 12 minutes. Taste and adjust the seasoning, if needed. The soup will thicken more as it cools.

4. Either use the soup in a recipe immediately, or transfer it to airtight containers and store in the refrigerator for up to 1 week or in the freezer.

Freezer Meal Instructions

TO FREEZE: Prepare and cool completely. Freeze in 1¼-cup portions in small freezable containers.

TO PREPARE FROM FROZEN: Thaw in the refrigerator or using the defrost setting of the microwave. Use in recipes as directed.

Cooking Notes

▶ You can substitute ½ teaspoon of poultry seasoning in place of the ¼ teaspoon thyme and ¼ teaspoon sage.

Recipe That Uses This Freezer Staple

▶ Cheesy Chicken and Stuffing Casserole (page 86)

CHICKEN BROTH

Making homemade chicken broth—actually, this one is more of a stock because of the use of bones and the long cooking time—is easy with very little hands-on time involved. Not only do you save money because you don't have to buy the boxed stuff, but the homemade stock itself is so much healthier for you. It's full of the iron, collagen, and vitamin-rich marrow from the bones. Don't get too caught up in having the exact right ingredients either. Below is a guideline of what you can put in your stock, but you can add or omit ingredients depending on what you have on hand. Yield: about 4 quarts (16 cups)

Leftover chicken bones and carcass

1 onion, quartered

2–3 carrots, chopped into a few pieces

3 ribs celery, chopped into a few pieces

1 cup chopped fresh parsley

2 cloves garlic, peeled

20 cups water

1. In a large stockpot, combine the chicken, onion, carrots, celery, parsley, garlic, and water. Bring to a boil over medium-high heat and then reduce the heat to a gentle simmer. Simmer, partially covered, for at least 4 hours, occasionally skimming off any foam that comes to the surface.

2. Using a strainer or slotted spoon, remove the solid contents, leaving just the chicken broth behind.

Freezer Meal Instructions

TO FREEZE: Let cool completely. Pour the broth into freezer-friendly Mason jars or freezer bags. Be sure to leave at least 1″ of headspace at the top of the jars.

TO PREPARE FROM FROZEN: Let the broth thaw in the refrigerator.

Recipes That Use This Freezer Staple

▶ Individual Chicken Pot Pies *(page 83)*

▶ Simple Homemade Stuffing *(page 87)*

▶ Totally Tasty Taco Kit *(page 108)*

▶ Shrimp Coconut Curry Bowls *(page 141)*

▶ Baked Chicken and Broccoli Alfredo *(page 150)*

▶ Tomato Bisque *(page 172)*

▶ Creamy Chicken, Veggie, and Wild Rice Soup *(page 183)*

▶ Classic Chicken Noodle Soup *(page 184)*

▶ Italian Sausage and Tortellini Soup *(page 186)*

▶ Cheeseburger Soup *(page 189)*

▶ French Dip Sandwiches *(page 198)*

▶ Rachel's Favorite Pot Roast *(page 200)*

▶ Curt's Slow Cooker Jambalaya *(page 203)*

▶ Polly's Signature Taco Soup *(page 209)*

Recipe Contributors

Several bloggers have influenced us over the years, including these five lovely, talented women. We were thrilled when they agreed to be a part of this project. Their recipes are killer and so are their Web sites. Be sure to swing by and get to know them!

JULIE BRASINGTON
FROM HAPPY HOME FAIRY

Contributed: **Mini Turkey and Veggie Cheeseburgers** *(page 127)*

Web site: **happyhomefairy.com**

Julie Brasington is the wife of a South Florida worship pastor, a mom of two busy boys, a preschool teacher, and a lover of (dark) chocolate chips. She is also the creator and author of Happy Home Fairy, a popular blog focused on encouraging and equipping moms to choose joy on the parenting journey. She shares easy craft ideas, *free* printables, simple recipes, corny jokes, holiday fun, thoughts on raising kids, and honest, heartfelt messages to uplift the weary mama.

MAUREEN WITMER
FROM TAKE THEM A MEAL

Contributed: **Creamy Butternut Squash Soup** *(page 177)*

Web site: **takethemameal.com**

Maureen is the director of outreach and engagement, as well as the recipe specialist, for Take Them a Meal, a free online tool designed to coordinate the delivery of meals. As a longtime user of the site, she was thrilled to join the team. After being diagnosed with celiac disease, Maureen has embraced gluten-free cooking. Her recipes and photographs can be found on the recipe section of Take Them a Meal. She and her husband, Andrew, live in Virginia, where she works from home and cares for their three young children.

KELLY SMITH
FROM THE NOURISHING HOME

Contributed: **Slow Cooker Sweet and Spicy Chicken** *(page 206)*

Web site: **thenourishinghome.com**

Kelly Smith loves the Lord, her family, and sharing her passion for gluten-free, whole food cooking and meal planning with others. She is a cookbook author and founder of The Nourishing Home— a popular gluten-free lifestyle blog dedicated to sharing delicious whole food recipes, meal plans, cooking tips, and encouragement. With a passion for masterfully transforming everyday comfort foods into delicious gluten-free creations, Kelly is on a mission to help individuals and families live a healthier, more nourished life.

CAMILLE STYLES

Contributed: **Sweet Potato and Black Bean Chili** *(page 181)*

Web site: **camillestyles.com**

On her award-winning site, Camille shares creative ideas for living a happy and healthy life. Her passion is to show readers approachable ways to elevate everyday moments. Camille is also the author of the bestselling book *Camille Styles Entertaining,* as well as a regular lifestyle contributor to numerous media outlets and national lifestyle brands.

ANN TIMM
FROM KEEPER OF THE HOME

Contributed: **Individual Chicken Pot Pies** *(page 83)*

Web site: **keeperofthehome.org**

Ann Timm is a Christ-follower, wife to an amazing man, and mama to six wonderful kiddos. She writes at Keeper of the Home, a site dedicated to naturally inspired living for homemakers, even as she drinks DIY bulletproof coffee and fanatically uses coconut oil for everything. Her husband, Mark, is CEO of ziglarfamily.com, and this has become another passion of hers. Ann juggles rural farm life, sports schedules, blended family dynamics, and working from home, but never without a prayer of thanksgiving for the many blessings she has.

Acknowledgments

This book is an extension of our blog, Thriving Home. Many years ago when we were floundering around with start-up costs and Web site kinks and figuring out how to run a blog authored by two people, we never could have imagined that we would one day be coauthoring a book in print. Our hearts are warmed by our followers—their feedback, their encouragement, and their enthusiasm. We simply would not be writing these words if it weren't for them. So to you, Thriving Home readers, thank you.

A huge thanks to our amazing, talented, driven, so-glad-she's-on-our-side literary agent, Maria Ribas. We would have fumbled clumsily through this whole process if it weren't for her. And to the amazing Rodale team: Dervla, Rae Ann, Angie, and all the other people behind the scenes who worked their tails off to turn our little dream into a reality.

To our husbands, for all the kid tag-teaming, kitchen cleaning, late night editing, date night brainstorming, and continual encouragement throughout our blogging years and cookbook writing process. You've done more behind-the-scenes work for this book than anyone will ever know.

To our pals Scott and Sam Myers for working their magic at our photo shoots. A special thanks to Sam for teaching us the harsh realities of what colors we should and shouldn't wear.

To the Haslags, Phillips, and Wamplers for letting us invade their homes, turn them into a micro-studio, and pretend they are ours for a day. We like your pretty things, and we're really thankful we didn't have to clean our own houses.

Thanks to our friends who gave up an afternoon to be in our photo shoots. You're so pretty. But a photo could never capture how beautiful you are inside and out.

To our parents. For always loving us unconditionally and being our #1 fans. There is no way to even summarize all the things we are thankful for. Just know we are so grateful for you and all you have done for us.

To our Recipe Testing Team. You all rock. Thanks for trusting us enough to try out recipes that were giving us fits and starts and for making this book better than we could on our own.

To the original Freezer Club gals. You were the genesis of this whole deal and paved the way for us to write this book. We are indebted especially to Darcie and Carla for their hard work to keep the group going for 7 years.

To MightyNest for the gobs of freezer containers you sent our way for the photo shoot.

To pesto. We wish we could have put you in every recipe. But, turns out you aren't good on pancakes. Alas, we love you.

Most of all, to the One who provided this opportunity. May this book be used for the good of many and to Your glory.

Index

Underscored page references indicate boxed text. **Boldfaced** page references indicate photographs.